SO-BSE-589

NEW DIRECTIONS FOR PROGRAM EVALUATION
A Publication of the American Evaluation Association

Nick L. Smith, *Syracuse University*
EDITOR-IN-CHIEF

Organizations in Transition: Opportunities and Challenges for Evaluation

Colleen L. Larson
Indiana University

Hallie Preskill
University of St. Thomas

EDITORS

Number 49, Spring 1991

JOSSEY-BASS INC., PUBLISHERS
San Francisco

ORGANIZATIONS IN TRANSITION: OPPORTUNITIES AND
 CHALLENGES FOR EVALUATION
Colleen L. Larson, Hallie Preskill (eds.)
New Directions for Program Evaluation, no. 49
Nick L. Smith, Editor-in-Chief

Microfilm copies of issues and articles are available in 16mm and 35mm,
as well as microfiche in 105mm, through University Microfilms Inc., 300
North Zeeb Road, Ann Arbor, Michigan 48106.

LC 85-644749   ISSN 0164-7989   ISBN 1-55542-795-2

NEW DIRECTIONS FOR PROGRAM EVALUATION is part of The Jossey-Bass
Education Series and is published quarterly by Jossey-Bass Inc., Publishers (publication number USPS 449-050).

EDITORIAL CORRESPONDENCE should be sent to the Editor-in-Chief,
Nick L. Smith, School of Education, Syracuse University, 330 Huntington
Hall, Syracuse, New York 13244-2340.

Printed on acid-free paper in the United States of America.

CONTENTS

EDITORS' NOTES

The days when American business leaders sold everything they produced are now little more than a nostalgic part of this country's economic history. In the 1970s, a far more eager and customer-focused Japan supplanted American industry as leaders in the world marketplace and sent a chill of fear through American business. Japan was soon followed by other countries that saw opportunities for capturing a share of the market, and collectively, these countries ended the chapter on U.S. domination in the world marketplace.

Today, American business organizations know that their products and services must be of high quality to compete in the world arena. Indeed, quality has become an obsession with many American business organizations. In an effort to increase their employees' motivation and productivity, business executives have adopted programs in total quality, quality control, and quality circles (Deming, 1981; Ouchi, 1981; Juran, 1978). They have also fought the challenge from foreign shores by purchasing powerful hardware and software systems, investing in high-speed production machines, and designing fully automated factories and warehouses. Yet as business leaders have moved forward with these investments and organization changes, the work force has lagged behind. Business leaders have assumed that state-of-the-art technology and quality circle programs could give them the competitive edge they so desperately need. However, many organizations do not have people with the necessary skills and motivation to participate in training for such initiatives as "just-in-time," statistical process control, high-tech innovations, or quality circles.

The increasing attempts of U.S. organizations to compete in a global economy have also led to unprecedented waves of mergers, acquisitions, and corporate restructuring. Evidence of the changing nature of business organizations is provided by Scott and Jaffe (1989, p. 1):

- In the past five years more than twelve thousand U.S. companies and corporate divisions have changed hands.
- Seventy percent of mergers end up as financial failures.
- The takeover trend is increasing. In 1989 it was more than double what is was in 1986.
- Companies expect to cut an average 15 percent of their work force.
- The hundred biggest mergers in the United States during a recent year affected four and a half million workers.

There is little doubt that American business organizations are in turmoil, and for the first time in our short industrial history, business executives are searching for answers to their steadily declining role in the world marketplace. These conditions have alerted business leaders to the need to do things differently and have created an atmosphere amenable to large-scale organizational change.

This volume introduces evaluators and other organization consultants to the complex realities of the changing world of business and industry as we see them. We hope to engage people not only in business organizations, but also in health care, education, government, and social services, in a critical dialogue about meeting the changing needs of organizations to bring about authentic change in their philosophy and practice. Evaluators and organization consultants play key roles in these efforts. We believe that as leaders strive to blaze new trails for improving their organizations, consultants must do the same. Toward that end, this volume includes several chapters intended to foster reflection on the nature of inquiry for organizations in transition. The authors of these chapters have backgrounds as diverse as the problems faced by organizations. We believe that this diversity deepens our understanding of the multiple viewpoints of those who think about, work with, and reflect upon evaluation in organizations.

Overview of the Chapters

The chapters in this volume are organized around two basic themes. Preskill's chapter sets the premise for the book. The three chapters by Tate and Cummings, Halpern, and Krueger then deal with how the practice of evaluation is changing in organizations in transition. The three chapters by Farley, Schwandt, and Larson look at evaluation from another perspective: its role in changing organizations.

In introducing the volume, Hallie Preskill in Chapter One argues that understanding an organization's culture, especially in times of change, is critical to understanding the utilization of evaluation information. While acknowledging that the research on evaluation utilization has been helpful, she says it has failed to consider the organizational context adequately. She calls on evaluators to uncover as many aspects of the organization's culture as possible—to view evaluation through a "cultural lens" so that evaluations may focus more sharply on utilization. In her conclusion, she uses examples to demonstrate how understanding elements of an organization's culture can help us understand the uses of evaluation.

In Chapter Two, Debra L. Tate and Oliver W. Cummings explain how evaluators can convince management of the importance of evaluation activities. As organizations strive to improve their own performance in ever-increasing competitive environments, evaluators must be seen as experts. Not only must they demonstrate an understanding of the client's business, but they must also know how to present an evaluation proposal that motivates the client to action. Tate and Cummings present a case example that illustrates their suggestions.

As another example of the need for evaluation in changing organizations, Edward S. Halpern, in Chapter Three, examines the growing complexity of product evaluation in high-tech industries. Organizations are finding that past practices in product evaluation are inadequate for solving the complex problems of high-tech environments. Halpern argues that product evaluation must occur at all stages of the product's life cycle from conceptualization to field testing if evaluation is to be valued as part of the production process. He also suggests that special attention should be given to the usability of high-tech products to ensure success in the marketplace.

In Chapter Four, Richard A. Krueger discusses how focus-group interviewing developed in the public sector has become increasingly used in private-sector organizations dealing with organizational change. He begins by providing a brief history of the use of the focus group and showing how the academic world has contributed to its development as a research and evaluation methodology. He then offers examples of how focus-group interviews have been used in government, health care, and business organizations. He concludes that American business and industry can obtain much valuable information from focus-group interviews.

The next three chapters represent a shift in focus from evaluation that occurs in changing organizations to evaluation that actually changes organizations. In Chapter Five, Joanne Farley explores the differences between the rationalist and sociotechnical frameworks and shows how they apply to organizational research and practice. She argues that the rationalist framework is inadequate for conducting research and evaluation in today's changing business environments. Indeed, she maintains that the predominant rationalist framework has become obsolete for conducting evaluations that are meaningful, fair, and socially responsible. She concludes by suggesting that the sociotechnical framework, though not the only alternative to the rationalist framework, shows great promise for the field of evaluation.

Thomas A. Schwandt's contribution in Chapter Six examines why moral analysis is not currently a practical force in evaluation or in business organizations. He shows that the difficulties of making moral practice central to our concerns in both evaluation and management are strikingly similar. He then poses the question "Can organizations be moral?" and presents developments that might make it possible to view organizations as moral agents, capable of organizing for both moral and economic purposes.

To sum up the evaluator's power to change organizations, Colleen L. Larson, in Chapter Seven, examines how evaluative inquiry can be used in analyzing efforts to transform management philosophy and practice. She argues that current evaluation practices are incapable of assessing the complexity of such initiatives. If we are to truly transform management philosophy and practice, she contends, we must explore the beliefs and interests that keep people grounded in traditional behavior. She urges evaluators to bring to the surface difficult issues that "undergird the dominant ideology that frames and molds the thoughts, dreams, aspirations, and expectations of people within the organization."

All of these chapters support the need to abandon traditional evaluation practices in favor of approaches designed to address the complex needs of business organizations. Business leaders are caught in a need to "ride the wave of change" (Morgan, 1986). We believe that evaluators and consultants can do much to calm the waters and work with organization leaders to create opportunities for a smoother ride.

Concluding Remarks

It is our hope that readers will find value in the questions posed, observations made, and the lessons documented throughout these chapters. Many of us have attempted to reframe our thinking about evaluation methodology and practice, but these are merely seeds for change. There is much yet to be learned about evaluation strategies for organizations in transition. We offer this volume in an effort to further critical dialogue about evaluation methodology that makes it possible for us to capture, interpret, and understand the complexity of the organizations that we collectively create.

Colleen L. Larson
Hallie Preskill
Editors

References

Deming, W. E. "What Top Management Must Do." *Business Week*, July 20, 1981, pp. 19–21.
Juran, J. M. "Japanese and Western Quality: A Contrast in Methods and Results." *Management Review*, 1978, *67*, 26–45.
Morgan, F. *Images of Organizations*. Newbury Park, Calif.: Sage, 1986.
Ouchi, W. G. *Theory Z: How American Business Can Meet the Japanese Challenge*. Reading, Mass.: Addison-Wesley, 1981.
Scott, C. D., and Jaffe, D. T. *Managing Organizational Change*. Los Altos, Calif.: Crisp Publications, 1989.

Colleen L. Larson joined the faculty in School Administration at Indiana University after having spent six years as an organization development and evaluation consultant to Fortune 500 companies. Her research and teaching focus on organization and change theory through interpretive and critical inquiry.

Hallie Preskill is assistant professor in the School of Education, Professional Psychology, and Social Work at the University of St. Thomas in St. Paul, Minnesota. Her research interests include evaluation theory, organizational culture, and the use of photography and metaphors in interpreting evaluation information.

The uses of evaluation must be understood from an organizational culture perspective. A case is made for grounding evaluation use within a cultural framework.

The Cultural Lens: Bringing Utilization into Focus

Hallie Preskill

Since Carol Weiss's (1966) call over two decades ago for a systematic study of conditions associated with utilization of evaluation results, much research has been conducted attempting to understand and explain how evaluation information is used. Arguing that the original image of "research utilization . . . embodies inappropriate imagery" (1981, p. 18), Weiss implored evaluators to build a cumulative body of research on evaluation use. Definitions of utilization have varied over the years. While Patton (1987) has written that until there is a universal definition of evaluation there will never be a universal definition of utilization, he does suggest that, from an accountability perspective, utilization means "intended use by intended users" (1988, p. 14). He explains that "we negotiate up front with intended users what an evaluation ought to achieve to make its benefits worth its costs" (p. 14). He has labeled this approach "utilization-focused evaluation" and defines it as "an approach that combines style and substance, activism and science, personal perspective and systematic information" (Patton, 1978, p. 290). Alkin (1990) has added that utilization "refers to the purposeful, planned consequences that result from applying evaluation information to a problem, question, or concern at hand" (p. 19).

Throughout the late 1970s and into the early 1980s, research on utilization focused primarily on two themes: types of use and factors that contribute to use. One category, which represents the traditional or "mainstream" type of use, has been called *instrumental* (Braskamp, 1982; Rich, 1977; Weiss, 1977) or *action use* (Alkin, 1985). This label suggests that the findings of the evaluation are put into direct, concrete, and observable use. In the second type, labeled *conceptual* use (Caplan, 1977; Patton, 1978;

Rich, 1977; Weiss, 1980), evaluation findings provide additional data to decision makers who then integrate it with information they have collected from other sources. In this case, evaluation may not lead to immediate action; rather, "conceptual use is manifested by changes in attitude and, where possible, in subsequent behavior" (Alkin, 1985, p. 21). Kennedy (1984) adds that "conceptual use is a formative process in which evidence is acted on by the user. It is sorted, sifted, and interpreted; it is transformed into implications and translated into inferences" (p. 225). The third category of use has been called *persuasive* (Rich, 1977; Leviton and Hughes, 1981), *symbolic* (Pelz, 1978; Young and Comptois, 1979), and *ritualistic* (Braskamp, 1980). Though each label implies a slight difference in interpretation, each reflects the influence of the evaluation's context on use. This type of utilization assumes a ritualistic or political application of the evaluation. Symbolic use is often a form of accountability that is meant to ensure the organization's survival.

The second stream of research has focused on the factors that lead to the use of evaluation information. In an attempt to assess the factors that influence evaluation use, Cousins and Leithwood (1986) conducted a literature search between the years 1971 and 1985 and found sixty-five empirical studies on evaluation use. From this study they discovered that twelve factors influence one or more types of use. Six of the factors are concerned with the *implementation* of evaluation: evaluation quality, credibility, relevance, communication, the findings themselves, and the timeliness of evaluations for users. The remaining six factors relate to the features of *policy settings:* information needs of users, decision characteristics, political climate, competing information, personal characteristics of users, and users' commitment and receptiveness to evaluation information (p. 359). Of particular interest, however, the authors found that the factors varied with the type of use. They explained that factors associated with policy settings were "more influential in affecting conceptual gains associated with evaluation results" (p. 360).

In spite of the many studies that have been conducted over the last twenty years or so, little research has focused specifically on the organizational context in which the evaluation takes place. Much of the research has defined independent variables at the micro level—such as the timeliness of the report, the evaluator's relationship to the organization, the political climate, or the decision maker's characteristics. For example, Alkin, Daillak, and White (1979) identified a category of factors that they labeled "organizational factors." These included relationships between site and district, site-level organizational arrangements, other information sources, teacher and staff views, student views, and costs and rewards. Yet research on evaluation use by Preskill (1984) in private-sector organizations, using the framework proposed by Alkin and colleagues, concluded "that the history of the organization, and its resultant culture, political environment and resources, provide an important context in which to view the factors that were found to directly influence evaluation use" (p. 266).

While much of the research on utilization has contributed greatly to our understanding of how evaluation information is used, the fact remains that the study of evaluation use has become fragmented and, in this author's opinion, has lost its grounding. There has been no unifying framework or theory tying together all that we know about use. In essence, it has failed to take into account the organization's context and, more specifically, the culture of the institution. Exceptions to this pattern can be seen in the work of Siegel and Tuckel (1985) and Faase and Pujdak (1987), who have written about the importance of the organization's beliefs and value systems, and the work of Kennedy (1984), who has studied the role of beliefs and myths in interpreting evaluation evidence. As we have come to understand types of use and the factors that contribute to instrumental and conceptual use, it is time to step back from the myriad of independent variables that have been studied and concentrate on the organizational context in which these factors emerge. By understanding an organization's culture, evaluators may be better prepared to conduct more useful evaluations. Building on Ott's (1989, p. vii) metaphor, evaluators would do well to "put on a different set of 'lenses' through which to 'see' an organization" in order to learn how evaluation information may be more fruitfully employed. This chapter explains how evaluation of all types may be used more fruitfully by examining the culture or the organization in which the evaluation occurs.

Organizations' Changing Environments

America's organizations have experienced revolutionary changes in the last ten years. One can hardly pick up a newspaper or talk with a colleague where the subject of reorganization, merger/consolidation, buyout, restructuring, or bankruptcy is not discussed. In a recent book, *When Giants Learn to Dance* (1989), Rosabeth Moss Kanter describes ways in which U.S. corporations must change to compete in the "global olympics." To illustrate the changing environment in which American businesses operate today, she uses an analogy based on the story of *Alice in Wonderland.* She explains that the croquet game in the story is

> a fictional game, nothing remains stable for very long, because everything is alive and changing around the player—an all-too-real condition for many managers. The mallet Alice uses is a flamingo, which tends to lift its head and face in another direction just as Alice tries to hit the ball. The ball, in turn, is a hedgehog, another creature with a mind of its own. Instead of lying there waiting for Alice to hit it, the hedgehog unrolls, gets up, moves to another part of the court, and sits down again. The wickets are card soldiers, ordered around by the Queen of

Hearts, who changes the structure of the game seemingly at whim by barking out an order to the wickets to reposition themselves around the court [p. 19].

Kanter completes the analogy by suggesting that if we substitute technology for the mallet, employees and customers for the hedgehog, and everyone from government regulators to corporate raiders for the Queen of Hearts, we then have a picture of the experience of a growing number of companies.

Reflecting on the mergers, acquisitions, and takeovers in the 1980s, Farrell and others (1990) report that by the end of the decade, $1.3 trillion was spent on "shuffling assets—on a par with the annual economic output of West Germany" (p. 52). This "shuffling" resulted in a "wave of corporate restructuring and merger mania" that created new expectations and demands on managers in dealing with "wrenching organizational change" (p. 52). Noting that "the magnitude of change impacting American industry in recent years has been staggering," Elliott (1990) discusses the effects of the downsizing and takeover trends in U.S. companies. He cautions readers to remember that organizational restructuring "signals a fundamental change in culture and strategy that sends shock waves throughout the organization." (p. 42).

Organizational Culture

Since the word *culture* was redefined by anthropologists over 100 years ago, scholars have failed to reach consensus about its meaning. Indeed, a study conducted by Kroeber and Kluckhohn (1952) identified 164 different definitions of culture. Nevertheless, many organizational analysts have identified a number of themes that are associated with culture. In the recent literature, Deal (1986) describes culture as "a closed circle of assumptions, beliefs, and understandings. . . . Culture is what keeps the herd moving west." He adds: "The bottom line of culture is to give meaning to a nonsensical world" (p. 27). In their often-cited book *Corporate Cultures,* Deal and Kennedy (1982) list five elements of culture: the business environment, values, heroes, rites and rituals, and the cultural network. Kilmann (1989) summarizes culture as shared values, beliefs, expectations, and norms. Norms, he explains, are the easiest to define. These are the unwritten rules of the game: "Don't disagree with the boss; don't rock the boat; don't share information with other groups" (p. 11). He adds that culture "is the social energy that moves the membership into action" (p. 11).

Edgar Schein (1985) has provided some of the most important work on organizational culture in the last decade. He defines culture as "a pattern of basic assumptions—invented, discovered, or developed by a given group as it learns to cope with its problems of external adaptation and internal integration—that has worked well enough to be considered valid and therefore to be taught to new members as the correct way to perceive, think, and feel in relation to those problems" (p. 9). Schein believes that culture is a product of group experience and that it is learned, evolves with new experiences, and can be changed. From what has been learned about organizational culture, Ott (1989, p. 68) suggests four functions of culture:

1. It provides shared patterns of cognitive interpretations or perceptions so organization members know how they are expected to act and think.
2. It provides shared patterns of affect, an emotional sense of involvement and commitment to organizational values and moral codes—of things worth working for and believing in—so organizational members know what they are expected to value and how they are expected to feel.
3. It defines and maintains boundaries, allowing identification of members and nonmembers.
4. It functions as an organizational control system, prescribing and prohibiting certain behaviors.

Schein (1985) has suggested that there are three levels of organizational culture: artifacts, values, and basic assumptions. Each of these characteristics may inform evaluators about the culture of the organization and may serve as contextual clues for conducting an evaluation with a focus on utilization. *Artifacts* include observations of physical space, the technological output of the group, its written and spoken language, its artistic productions, and the overt behavior of its members. *Values* reflect the organization's sense of what "ought" to be. Values are often embodied in an organization's ideology or philosophy. Deal and Kennedy (1982) write that "values are the bedrock of any corporate culture. As the essence of a company's philosophy for achieving success, values provide a sense of common direction for all employees and guidelines for their day-to-day behavior" (p. 21). The *basic assumptions* of an organization are the beliefs that have become integrated into the behavior of its members and are so taken for granted that they are often implicit and, according to Schein, "nonconfrontable and nondebatable" (p. 18). This concept is similar to Argyris's (1976) notion of theories-in-use, which refers to the implicit assumptions that guide behavior and inform group members how to perceive, think, and feel about things. According to Schein, these basic assumptions involve humanity's relationship to nature, the nature of reality and truth, the nature of human nature, the nature of human activity, and the nature of human relations (p. 86).

Uncovering Culture Within an Organization

Organizational analysts have used various methods to decode an organization's culture. The search for symbols within an organizational culture has been one theme on which researchers have focused. Smircich (1985) suggests that research focusing on symbols would look for the words, ideas, and constructs that impel, legitimate, coordinate, and realize organized activity in specific settings. "How do they accomplish the task?" and "Whose interests are they serving?" are typical questions (p. 67). Pettigrew (1983) has used the method of social dramas or critical events to look at the growth, evolution, transformation, and decay of an organization over time. Others have listened to the organizational stories, myths, metaphors, and sagas. (See Beck and Moore, 1985; Clark, 1972; Deal and Kennedy, 1982; Krefting and Frost, 1985; Myrsiades, 1987; Peters and Waterman, 1982; Pondy, 1983; Tommerup, 1988.) Still others have recommended studying the organization's rites, rituals, and ceremonies. (See Deal and Kennedy, 1982; Harris and Sutton, 1986; Trice and Beyer, 1984.)

Schein (1986) cautions that in studying organizational values, it is imperative that analysts be able to uncover the tacit, unconscious assumptions of reality and truth. At the same time, Ott (1989) explains that culture is a concept, not a single truth, and that our methods for uncovering and understanding culture must "break out of the information systems/logical-positivist/quasi-experimental mold that has placed a mental and emotional straitjacket on organizational theory and theorists for too many years" (p. ix). Ott's major concern is that quantitative, quasi-experimental research methods cannot adequately measure "unconscious, virtually forgotten basic assumptions" (p. 3). Some organizational analysts, however, have broken away from the structuralist and systems perspectives and have used a qualitative, interpretive, or phenomenological approach to study culture. These researchers have chosen this paradigm because the data typically produce "thick descriptions" (Geertz, 1973) that "allow ambiguities, contradictions, and paradoxes to be explored with relative ease" (Siehl and Martin, 1988). Berger (1986) maintains that "the study of organizational culture demands a search for subtle meanings—not simply artifacts (such as architecture, stories, heroes, ceremonies, policies) that are supposed to represent the latent culture" (p. 52). Schein (1985) recommends the use of an iterative "clinical" interview, which he describes as "a series of encounters and joint explorations between the investigator and various motivated informants who live in the organization and embody its culture" (p. 112). He further suggests a ten-step model for revealing an organization's culture.

Some researchers have developed a "hybrid" measure of culture by first collecting qualitative data in the form of observations, in-depth interviews, and archival data to understand the culture and then using the qualitative data to construct a questionnaire that results in quantitative data. According to Siehl and Martin (1988), this approach is particularly valuable if the goal is to compare organizational cultures with one another.

Implications for Evaluation

Understanding an organization's culture can provide the evaluator with critical information about the nature of the business and the activities within the organization. For example, Glidewell's (1986) research on the assumptions about training in corporate cultures suggests that human resource development professionals would do well to learn about the "network of linked assumptions about training and how it is done in the corporation" if they wish their activities to be valued (p. 47). In Faase and Pujdak's (1987) evaluation for a religious congregation, the value of understanding a group's culture became clear. In developing various data collection instruments they discovered that "the evaluator's familiarity with the value systems of church groups and religious communities provided an indispensable background and framework within which to ask appropriate questions" (p. 78). They conclude that because of their attention to culture, and the group's involvement with all phases of the evaluation, "the report had a compelling presence in the chapter due to shared understanding" (p. 80). For Kilmann (1989, p. 11), the fundamental question is: "Does the organization's culture support the behavior that is needed for organizational success today?" All of these comments reflect the necessity of grounding research and evaluation in the organization's culture.

How, then, can evaluators link an organization's culture with the use of evaluation information? Evaluators seeking to understand an organization's culture must look for the values and underlying assumptions of the organization in terms of both individual and group behavior. For example, how does the organization define "truth" or determine what is real? Does the company solve its problems through creative conflict and discussion (believing this approach to be effective and productive)? Or do its differing assumptions about the nature of truth lead it to avoid conflict and defer many decisions to perceived experts or those in authority? Illustrating this point, Schein (1985) relates how in one organization the memos he had circulated to stimulate ideas never got to certain managers unless he presented them personally. He later discovered that unsolicited ideas were not welcomed in this culture—ideas were considered only when asked for because, in this organization, unsolicited information was seen as a challenge to other information sources that could be perceived as not doing their jobs. This element of culture directly relates to the "evaluation reporting" and "user characteristics" factors cited by Alkin (1985).

Another example can be seen in an organization in which I am currently providing evaluation services. In preliminary discussions with the client, I learned that the organization is evolving from a time-oriented culture, where all processes of employees are timed (reminiscent of scientific management and Taylorism), to one that has been described as sociotechnical. (For an excellent overview of this paradigm, see Joanne Farley's chapter in this volume.) In managing processes rather than the work of individual people, this company's cultural change relates to Schein's (1985) underlying assumptions of culture labeled the "nature of human activity." These assumptions determine what is acceptable behavior in the work environment. Organizational assumptions regarding the nature of human activity also provide the underpinnings of managerial decision-making. When these assumptions allow employees wide latitude in expressing their views openly, a more participatory style of decision making is likely to emerge. As Schein (1985, p. 103) explains, "If members of a given organization have different assumptions about the nature of work activity, and its relative importance to other activities, those differences will manifest themselves in frustration and communication breakdowns." In my example, the organization is moving from a time orientation that results in quantitative evaluation information to a process orientation that will result in more qualitative data. This paradigmatic shift is of great concern to training program evaluators. Decision makers who are more familiar with quantitative data may be reluctant to base their decisions on qualitative data. Thus evaluators interested in how their findings are used must determine what kinds of data will be "believable" within the changing organization's culture. In this example, the evaluation factor "evaluation procedures" (Alkin, 1985) may be better understood within this organizational culture perspective.

Although evaluators will probably not be able to carry out in-depth cultural analyses in many of their evaluations, they can attempt to find out the organization's basic assumptions about itself, about reality, about the nature of time and how it is structured, about the nature of space and its symbolic meanings, about the relationship of people to each other, and about the assumptions underlying management practices. Evaluators can accomplish this by listening to the stories, myths, and metaphors people use to tell about the organization and its history, by identifying the organization's heroes and heroines, by observing the organization's rites, rituals, and celebrations, and by examining behavioral norms.

Conclusion

Previous research on evaluation utilization, particularly the factors leading to use, have in all likelihood improved evaluation practice. Criticizing this research, however, Patton (1987) writes: "Indeed, most of the research on utilization has focused on identifying the factors that contribute to use rather than on variations in utilization itself" (p. 112). In one interpretation, Patton's statement may be seen as a suggestion to frame utilization within an organizational context—to focus on the particulars of the organization and the individual client values and assumptions in order to maximize the use of evaluation data.

The research on evaluation utilization has also contributed much to our understanding that there are many kinds of use in addition to the immediate application of evaluation findings to program decisions. Asserting that conceptual use is taking place in organizations and that it does lead to program reform, Alkin (1990) writes: "Decision makers report that they value research and evaluation findings because they provide news; they alert people to new ideas; they show alternative ways of thinking about problems; they alter what is taken for granted as inevitable and what is seen as subject to change" (p. 22).

Lest some readers be concerned that organizational culture is just another fad that will fade away as have many other hot topics, Kilmann, Saxton, and Serpa (1986) suggest that corporate culture is too important to be dismissed as another fad. They believe that "culture is the social energy that drives—or fails to drive—the organization" (p. 92). "What goes on in an organization," they say, "is guided by the cultural qualities of shared meaning, hidden assumptions, and values that will guide evaluators toward conducting utilization-focused evaluations. Culture provides a necessary framework for making sense of the multiple realities that exist in every organization. It is the critical lens that helps evaluators see what strategies should be used in an evaluation to increase its potential use, and it provides the context in which to understand the many factors found to influence evaluation utilization. In short, the organizational culture perspective provides a new approach for analyzing organizational behavior and thus has a direct impact on the uses of evaluation.

References

Alkin, M. C. A Guide for Evaluation Decision Makers. Newbury Park, Calif: Sage, 1985.

Alkin, M. C. Debates on Evaluation. Newbury Park, Calif: Sage, 1990.

Alkin, M. C., Daillak, R., and White, P. Using Evaluations: Does Evaluation Make a Difference? Newbury Park, Calif: Sage, 1979.

Argyris, C. "Theories of Action That Inhibit Learning." American Psychologist, 1976, 39, 638-654.

Beck, B.E.F., and Moore, L. F. "Linking the Host Culture to Organizational Variables." In P. J. Frost, L. F. Moore, M. R. Louis, C. C. Lundberg, and J. Martin (eds.), Organizational Culture. Newbury Park, Calif: Sage, 1985.

Berger, M. A. "Research on Corporate Culture: The Agony and the Ecstasy." In J. C. Glidewell (ed.), Corporate Cultures: Research Implications for Human Resource Development. Alexandria, Va.: American Society for Training and Development, 1986.

Braskamp, L. A. "Assessing the Utilization of a Program Evaluation: A Review." Paper presented at the Conference on Planning and Conducting Program Evaluations and Reviews in Higher Education, St. Petersburg, Florida, 1980.

Braskamp, L. A. "A Definition of Use." Studies in Educational Evaluation, 1982, 8, 169-174.

Caplan, N. "A Minimal Set of Conditions Necessary for the Utilization of Social Science Knowledge in Policy Formation at the National Level." In C. H. Weiss (ed.), *Using Social Research in Public Policy Making*. Lexington, Mass.: Levington-Heath, 1977.

Clark, B. R. "The Organizational Saga in Higher Education." *Administrative Science Quarterly*, 1972, *17* (2), 178–184.

Cousins, J. B., and Leithwood, K. A. "Current Empirical Research on Evaluation Utilization." *Review of Educational Research*, 1986, *56* (3), 331–364.

Deal, T. E. "Deeper Culture: Mucking, Muddling, and Metaphors." In J. C. Glidewell (ed.), *Corporate Cultures: Research Implications for Human Resource Development*. Alexandria, Va.: American Society for Training and Development, 1986.

Deal, T. E., and Kennedy, A. A. *Corporate Cultures*. Reading, Mass.: Addison-Wesley, 1982.

Elliot, R. D. "The Challenge of Managing Change." *Personnel Journal*, 1990, *69* (3), 40–49.

Faase, T. P., and Pujdak, S. "Shared Understanding of Organizational Culture." In J. Nowakowski (ed.), *The Client Perspective on Evaluation*. New Directions for Program Evaluation, no. 36. San Francisco: Jossey-Bass, 1987.

Farrell, C., Schiller, Z., Zellner, W., Hof, R., and Schroeder, M. "The Best and Worst Deals of the 1980s." *Business Week*, January 15, 1990, pp. 52–62.

Geertz, C. *The Interpretation of Cultures*. New York: Basic Books, 1973.

Glidewell, J. C. "Assumptions About Training in Some Corporate Cultures." In J. C. Glidewell (ed.), *Corporate Cultures: Research Implications for Human Resource Development*. Alexandria, Va.: American Society for Training and Development, 1986.

Harris, S. G., and Sutton, R. I. "Functions of Parting Ceremonies in Dying Organizations." *Academy of Management Journal*, 1986, *28* (1), 5–30.

Kanter, R. M. *When Giants Learn to Dance*. New York: Simon & Schuster, 1989.

Kennedy, M. M. "How Evidence Alters Understanding and Decisions." *Educational Evaluation and Policy Analysis*, 1984, *6* (3), 207–226.

Kilmann, R. H. "A Completely Integrated Program for Creating and Maintaining Organizational Success." *Organizational Dynamics*, 1989, *18* (1), 5–19.

Kilmann, R. H., Saxton, M. J., and Serpa, R. "Issues in Understanding and Changing Culture." *California Management Review*, 1986, *28* (2), 87–94.

King, J. A., and Pechman, E. M. *The Process of Evaluation in Local School Settings*. New Orleans, La.: Tulane University, 1982.

Krefting, L. A., and Frost, P. J. "Untangling Webs, Surfing Waves, and Wildcatting." In P. J. Frost, L. F. Moore, M. R. Louis, C. C. Lundberg, and J. Martin (eds.), *Organizational Culture*. Newbury Park, Calif.: Sage, 1985.

Kroeber, A. L., and Kluckhohn, C. *Culture: A Critical View of Concepts and Definitions*. New York: Vintage Books, 1952.

Leviton, L. C., and Hughes, E.F.X. "Research on the Utilization of Evaluations: A Review and Synthesis." *Evaluation Review*, 1981, *5* (4), 525–548.

Myrsiades, L. S. "Corporate Stories as Cultural Communications in the Organizational Setting." *Management Communication Quarterly*, 1987, *1* (1), 84–120.

Ott, J. S. *The Organizational Culture Perspective*. Chicago: Dorsey Press, 1989.

Patton, M. Q. *Utilization-Focused Evaluation*. Newbury Park, Calif.: Sage, 1978.

Patton, M. Q. "Evaluation's Political Inherency: Practical Implications for Design and Use." In D. Palumbo (ed.), *The Politics of Program Evaluation*. Newbury Park, Calif.: Sage, 1987.

Patton, M. Q. "The Evaluator's Responsibility for Utilization." *Evaluation Practice*, 1988, *9* (2), 5–24.

Pelz, D. C. "Some Expanded Perspectives on the Use of Social Science in Public Policy." In J. M. Yinger and S. J. Cutler (eds.), *Major Social Issues: A Multidisciplinary View*. New York: Free Press, 1978.

Peters, T. J., and Waterman, R. H. *In Search of Excellence.* New York: Harper & Row, 1982.

Pettigrew, A. M. "On Studying Organizational Cultures." In J. Van Maanen (ed.), *Qualitative Methodology.* Newbury Park, Calif.: Sage, 1983.

Pondy, L. R. "The Role of Metaphors and Myths in Organization and in the Facilitation of Change." In L. R. Pondy, P. J. Frost, G. Morgan, and T. C. Dandridge (eds.), *Organizational Symbolism.* Greenwich, Conn.: JAI Press, 1983.

Preskill, H. "Evaluation Use in the Management/Supervisory Training Programs of Banking Organizations." Unpublished doctoral dissertation, University of Illinois at Champaign–Urbana, 1984.

Rich, R. F. "Uses of Social Science Information by Federal Bureaucrats: Knowledge of Action Versus Knowledge for Understanding." In C. E. Weiss (ed.), *Using Social Research in Public Policy Making.* Lexington, Mass.: Lexington-Heath, 1977.

Schein, E. H. *Organizational Culture and Leadership.* San Francisco: Jossey-Bass, 1985.

Schein, E. H. "Deep Culture." In J. C. Glidewell (ed.), *Corporate Cultures: Research Implications for Human Resource Development.* Alexandria, Va.: American Society for Training and Development, 1986.

Siegel, K., and Tuckel, P. "The Utilization of Evaluation Research: A Case Analysis." *Evaluation Review,* 1985, *9* (3), 307–328.

Siehl, C., and Martin, J. "Measuring Organizational Culture: Mixing Qualitative and Quantitative Methods." In M. Owens, M. Moore, and R. C. Snyder (eds.), *Inside Organizations.* Newbury Park, Calif.: Sage, 1988.

Smircich, L. "Is the Concept of Culture a Paradigm for Understanding Organizations and Ourselves?" In P. J. Frost, L. F. Moore, M. R. Louis, C. C. Lundberg, and J. Martin (eds.), *Organizational Culture.* Newbury Park, Calif.: Sage, 1985.

Tommerup, P. "From Trickster to Father Figure." In M. Owens, M. Moore, and R. C. Snyder (eds.), *Inside Organizations.* Newbury Park, Calif.: Sage, 1988.

Trice, H. M., and Beyer, J. M. "Studying Organizational Cultures Through Rites and Ceremonials." *Academy of Management Review,* 1984, *9* (4), 653–669.

Weiss, C. H. "Utilization of Evaluation: Toward Comparative Study." Paper presented at the American Sociological Association meeting, Miami, Florida, September 1, 1966.

Weiss, C. H. "Introduction." In C. H. Weiss (ed.), *Using Social Research in Public Policy Making.* Lexington, Mass.: Lexington-Heath, 1977.

Weiss, C. H. *Three Terms in Search of Reconceptualization: Knowledge, Utilization, and Decision-Making.* Cambridge, Mass.: Huron Institute, 1980.

Weiss, C. H. "Measuring the Use of Evaluation." In J. Ciarlo (ed.), *Utilizing Evaluation.* Newbury Park, Calif: Sage, 1981.

Young, C. J., and Comptois, J. "Increasing Congressional Utilization of Evaluation." In F. Zweig (ed.), *Evaluation in Legislation.* Newbury Park, Calif: Sage, 1979.

Hallie Preskill is assistant professor in the School of Education, Professional Psychology, and Social Work at the University of St. Thomas in St. Paul, Minnesota. Her research interests include evaluation theory, organizational culture, and the use of photography and metaphors in interpreting evaluation information.

Promoting evaluations with management requires not only technical competence in evaluation, but outstanding persuasion skills as well.

Promoting Evaluations with Management

Debra L. Tate, Oliver W. Cummings

The changes occurring in business today have an effect not only on the way business is conducted and with whom, but on organizational structures, corporate cultures, and what is required of people in organizations. Increasing customer expectations, intensifying foreign competition, changing population demographics, expansion into more global markets, the need for culturally sensitive business acumen—such changes have profound impacts on all segments of our work environments. Technological change will continue to alter the way in which work is performed. Quality and productivity will continue to receive intense scrutiny by management.

As human resource management departments seek to improve organizational performance in these ever-changing environments, the need for evaluation work increases as does the opportunity to promote it. Evaluation professionals must be able to communicate the importance and organizational benefits of program, process, or product evaluation if they are to promote their services in the business setting. This chapter delineates the evaluation and persuasion skills needed to position evaluation appropriately to meet the changing needs of organizations.

Selling: An Evaluator Skill

Evaluators ultimately sell a service. They must sell more frequently and more effectively than many other professionals. They must sell clients on the idea of evaluation and on specific proposals and designs; they must sell people on the value of participating in the evaluation study; they sell reports, results, and conclusions; and when they have completed one project, they must often sell the next one. The tangible product that evaluators sell—evaluation findings—is a relatively minor part of the service they provide. In selling, evaluators must communicate the value-added product of the evaluation. That product is the appropriate recommendation or the public certification of value.

In selling evaluations, the evaluator must be an expert and be seen as an expert, demonstrate understanding of the client's business, and present the proposal in a way that motivates the client to appropriate action. These activities can be applied conceptually to an organization, a collection of stakeholders, or an individual buyer.

Be an Expert and Be Seen as an Expert. The evaluator must know the product or service—whether it is a needs assessment, performance test, formative course evaluation, or impact study. That is, evaluators must be recognized as having special skills that allow them to perform such services better than anyone else. Evaluators must also know how their product and service can benefit clients. Clients want to trust the evaluator to do the right things in the process of evaluating. They also want the evaluator to help them understand the benefits of the evaluation to their work and their business.

Instead of discussing the benefits of a service, evaluators often focus on describing its features. For example, the benefit of a training needs assessment is not the identification of training needs; those are *results* of the assessment. The benefits of the evaluation are satisfied participants (since training is targeted to meet specific organizational and individual needs) and reduced training costs (since participants are trained only on essential skills and not those that are merely desirable). In human services, the benefits might be creation of a socially responsible program or the politically defensible allocation of public resources.

A benefit is the satisfaction of a client's key need or want. To the client, the benefits of evaluation may not be obvious. In initial meetings with the client, the evaluator must listen attentively to understand the client's language (code words) and frame of reference. As the evaluator begins to understand the client's needs, his or her efforts must be translated into a form that satisfies those needs. Thus the evaluator must be able to articulate both the benefits and the links to the client's needs.

Table 1 illustrates the differences between an evaluation's benefits and its features. Evaluators must understand and be able to communicate these benefits and features if they are to build trust and earn the respect, and the business, of the client. To focus on those benefits of your service that meet your clients' needs, however, you must know your clients and their business.

Demonstrate Understanding of the Client's Business. A first step in establishing yourself as a trusted adviser is to demonstrate an understanding of the client's business or industry. This will require some fluency in the financial and operational language of the business. It also necessitates

Table 1. Differences Between Benefits and Features

Benefit	Related Features
Eliminate or reduce costs	In needs assessment: Focusing the intervention on actual need reduces development, production, and delivery costs and increases productivity of employees. (Well-trained or well-supported employees are more efficient.)
	In formative evaluation: Systematic assessment minimizes the number of review and revision cycles necessary to achieve a finished product, thus reducing development costs.
	In testing for outcomes: Measuring outcomes gives assurance that expected performance changes have been achieved, thus reducing subsequent retraining needs. If tests are used to exempt personnel from portions of training, the savings in training time can also be claimed.
	In follow-up: Assessing the intervention's performance in the field ensures that only functional products or programs are left in place. This ensures that participant time and maintenance efforts associated with the product are justified.
Assure quality; know that the investment continues to be justified	In needs assessment: Matching the needs assessment approach (for example, analytic, discrepancy, democratic, or diagnostic—see Stufflebeam and others, 1985—or some other taxonomy) to the fundamental questions assures that the study will produce on-target results that can be translated to high-quality follow-on products.
	In formative evaluation and testing for outcomes: Validating fulfillment of the intervention's objectives and proper execution of approaches satisfies a short-term quality assurance need. Providing an objective assessment ensures that the team's blind spots do not allow problems to go unnoticed.
	In follow-up: Quality assurance can be achieved by systematically confirming the transfer of the intervention's outcomes to the job or confirming that the intervention had the desired impact on the business problem through accurate data gathering and reproducible interpretation and conclusions.
Improve or protect the client's reputation	In needs assessment: Positive reactions to the intervention can be ensured by sound sampling procedures, realistic study design, and links with other important systems that are affected.
	In formative evaluation: The client's reputation is less likely to be damaged by the intervention when the evaluation points out its key strengths and weaknesses. This can be accomplished through a disciplined inquiry into the characteristics and effects of the intervention and subsequently enhancing the strengths and addressing the weaknesses before release to the field.

Table 1. *(continued)*

Benefit	Related Features
	In follow-up: A reputation for relevance and quality should be maintained since systematic follow-up helps to ensure that valuable interventions are left in the field and justifies elimination of products or programs that do not yield the expected benefits.
Shorten the time between problem and solution	In needs assessment: Doing it right the first time requires less time and effort than redoing segments. Defining audience characteristics, job responsibilities, tasks and associated knowledge, and attitudinal and skill needs for employees leads to a detailed, focused approach to the follow-on work.
	In formative evaluation: Because data regarding strengths and weaknesses are collected systematically as portions of the intervention are implemented on a trial basis, changes can be made during product or program development. This strategy is preferable to waiting until the finished product is available, testing it, and then redoing major (or minor) segments.
	In testing for outcomes: When the intervention is a training program, the development of tests and performance measures prior to the preparation of content provides a clear blueprint for the subject matter experts. This obliges the specialist to focus on the important aspects of content and prevents the inclusion of superficial or irrelevant content. Thus, the time required for writing/rewriting and for review of content is reduced.
	In follow-up: Follow-up studies often serve as the basis for establishing a new level of needs assessment by identifying what does and does not work. Thus, problems may be identified earlier and defined more clearly before they reach crisis proportions. This enables the team to react faster to solve problems.

an understanding of the client's life cycle growth (is the business a startup, or is it mature?), business strategy, and industry trends. Finally, it will require some knowledge of the political, economic, and environmental forces affecting the client.

Equally important, the evaluator must view problems and opportunities from the client's perspective. This means presenting solutions in business terms that the client understands. Since clients have their own jargon, evaluators must learn to adapt their mode of communication to the client's language.

An evaluator must have a bottom-line orientation and tie recommendations to the client's business or strategic plan. This will require an understanding of the client's strategic success factors and necessitates aligning the evaluation outcomes to these success factors. The ultimate goal of the evaluator should be to demonstrate how he or she will add value to the client's business.

Clients come with predispositions, beliefs, and biases about themselves, about the object of the evaluation, about the evaluator or evaluation team, and about the need for evaluation. Clients also have priorities that may or may not be stated. Most clients have experience in data gathering and interpretation, which needs to be acknowledged and built upon. They look to the evaluator for what they cannot do themselves. Clients must help the evaluator to identify those needs.

Most clients want creativity in the evaluator's solutions. At the same time, they always assess proposals for realism and practicality. The evaluator must determine how much clients know and what they believe about the proposed evaluation.

The evaluator must understand their clients' motives, at some level, in order to deal with their personal quirks in making decisions. Mangan (1964) lists six blocks to persuasion: suspicion, inertia, fear, pride, incompetence (or, we would add, ignorance), and jealousy. All of these, as well as preconceptions, timing, and economics, can interfere with acceptance of a proposed evaluation. Each of these factors should be weighed as the evaluator tries to assess the client's reactions to the proposed evaluation. It is through this context that statements of benefits can be made most persuasively.

Motivate the Client to Take Appropriate Action. Planning and preparation are essential to success. Here are some concrete suggestions:

Make your primary idea a specific, clear statement of the actions you recommend. Say to yourself, for example, "When I finish presenting this proposal, I want my client to agree to set up a series of specific interviews, name a committee to advise us in the conduct of this evaluation, approve the drafting of a sampling plan and survey instruments . . ."
Identify common ground; use the client's beliefs in preparing your presentation. To the extent you can, take the client's frame of reference. Connect your goals with the client's major business strategies and needs.
Start with facts the client knows, and answer the client's questions before they are asked. Address both supporting and contradictory evidence for your position, and always lead to ideas that strengthen your position.
Seek acceptance of your ideas and goals. Demonstrate flexibility in terms of fine-tuning or changing your goals to take advantage of opportunities or adjust to new priorities.
Create a positive tone. It is not enough merely to present data to support your position—you need to *interpret* data to reflect the client's situation and *show* the client how the facts are important to the type of evaluation you are promoting.

It is important, too, to order your ideas and presentation:

Start with "The Big Idea" and immediately tell your client why he or she should listen to you. The reason the client should listen to you is best expressed as the most significant benefit he or she will gain from your service. "If I told you this evaluation could save you as much as $2 million in training time, wouldn't you want to know more about what we are proposing?"

Elaborate on that first benefit. Specify how it is derived, and tie it to key features of the evaluation you have proposed.

Present additional benefits (in order of their importance), and elaborate on them. Show the client how the evaluation produces the claimed benefits.

Anticipate the client's objections and deal with them. Present the potential objection and, to the extent possible, disarm it. This means you must have a thorough understanding of your proposal and its ramifications in the client's business, as well as anticipating any concerns the client might raise.

Summarize by going back to the overall idea and the one or two key benefits.

Don't forget to ask for the work. Clients want to buy from providers who want to serve their needs. End with specific action steps for the client—for example, have the client set up a meeting, make a decision, or name a project team.

A Case Example

To make these suggestions clearer, we have developed a case example that illustrates these ideas. This case demonstrates the planning concerns and approaches that were taken in promoting a curriculum needs assessment in the tax practice of our organization, Arthur Andersen & Co. In a dynamic business environment, one must be aware of all the factors that can affect the business. Economics, legislative changes, demographic shifts— all need to be examined thoroughly to understand the business. In the present case, we examined all these factors and then developed an approach that was appropriate, given the business needs. The rationale for undertaking the project was broadly divided into two areas: external issues and internal issues.

Two external issues had a significant impact on the project: major changes in legislation that affected the ways in which personnel did their jobs and major changes in demographics that increased the diversity of personnel being recruited by the division. There were four internal issues supporting the need for a curriculum planning effort. First, some of the division's service lines had reached their peak in terms of growth and were beginning to level off. Thus there was a need to explore new service lines, which required new personnel skills. Second, the division had made considerable investment in software development, and there was a need to determine the extent of software use and personnel training requirements. Third, the division was exploring more efficient means of completing compliance (tax return preparation and planning) work, and there was a need to determine how these new initiatives might affect the training requirements of personnel. Fourth, there was a need to determine whether the appropriate training was being delivered to the proper personnel at the optimal point in their careers.

After identifying the major issues affecting the business, the next step in the selling approach was to specify how the project would address these issues and to outline the benefits the division would realize as a result. To do this, it was important to understand the success factors of the division. In reviewing the success factors, we were able to glean some information regarding the operational results the division hoped to achieve.

We then examined each service line within the division to determine its growth potential. In doing this, we used Porter's (1980) life cycle model, which posits that a business goes through four phases: emergence, growth, maturity, and decline or resurgence (see Figure 1). Once we determined each service line's stage in its life cycle, we were able to specify the operational variables we needed to track for that service line. These variables depended on the service line's stage in its life cycle. In a mature service line, for example, leverage ratios—the number of staff supervised by each partner

Figure 1. The Life Cycle Model

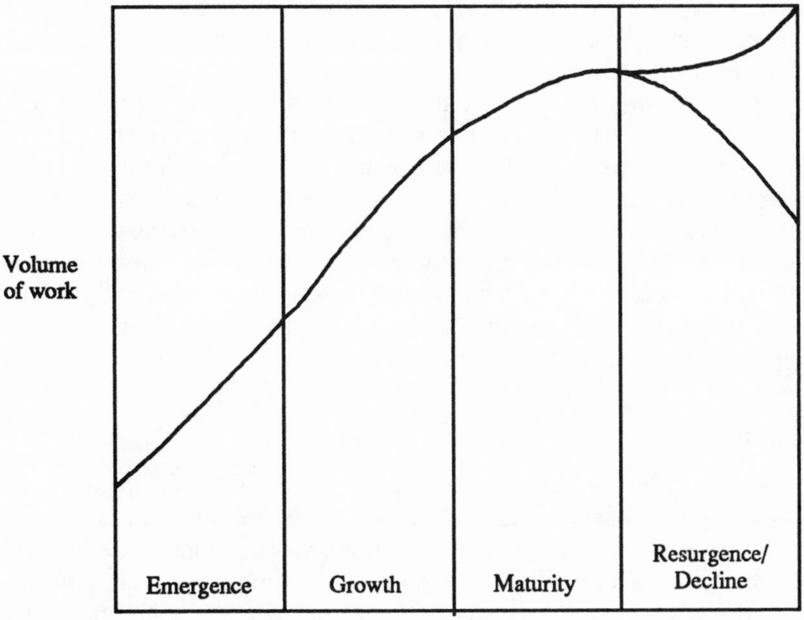

Volume
of work

| Emergence | Growth | Maturity | Resurgence/ Decline |

Source: Porter (1980).

on average—are one operational result that can be linked to training. In an emerging service line, entrepreneurial activity, comfort level, and actual promotion of a new service (for example, developing methodologies and submitting proposals) are operational results that can be linked to training. By examining factors such as these for each service line, we were able to determine how much additional growth in each service line was likely. We then used this information to target our curriculum planning efforts to those service lines that had the highest potential payback for the firm.

Once the variables to be tracked were identified, the next step in selling the curriculum plan to management was to demonstrate clearly how the project would affect the variables and how this would benefit the organization. This required providing the link between the curriculum plan and the operational results important to the division. In doing this, it was necessary to establish a series of causal links. Since the firm operates in a constantly changing environment, it was not possible to establish true cause-and-effect relationships; instead, we provided sufficient evidence to suggest a causal link between a series of variables.

In the present case, we attempted to link the goals of the curriculum to the operational results that were directly related to the tax division's strategic goals. For example, we knew that the tax division had a service line in the growth phase and that they expected chargeable hours to increase by 20 percent over the next year. One way the tax division could improve its ability to meet this goal was to provide training to selected personnel who did not currently have the required skills to perform effectively in this service line.

By specifying performance-based goals in our training program, we were able to establish the link between the training outcome and the operational results—that is, chargeable hours. In gathering performance data to support these links, we verified that personnel did not have the knowledge or skills prior to training, that they did have the required knowledge at the conclusion of the training, and that the information had transferred to the job. By demonstrating the logic underlying each link and providing hard performance measures to support each link, the causal chain was established to predict a positive change in the operational results.

Summary

A key to improving organizational performance today is recognizing and addressing the changing needs of organizations and the abilities of people to meet them. As the need to improve organizational performance increases, so too does the opportunity to promote evaluation work. As evaluation professionals, we must stress to our clients the organizational benefits to be realized in conducting program, process, or product evaluations. In selling evaluations, the evaluator needs to be recognized as an expert, to demonstrate understanding of the client's business, and to present the proposal in a way that motivates the client to appropriate action. The case study presented here illustrates each of these steps in the context of a curriculum planning effort in a large service organization.

References

Mangan, J. T. *What a Salesman Should Know About Selling Himself.* Chicago: Dartnell Corp., 1964.
Porter, M. E. *Competitive Strategies: Techniques for Analyzing Industries and Corporations.* New York: Free Press, 1980.
Stufflebeam, D. L., McCormick, C. H., Brinkerhoff, R. O., and Nelson, C. O. *Conducting Educational Needs Assessment.* Boston: Kluwer-Nijhoff, 1985.

Debra L. Tate is an experienced senior in the Evaluation Services Unit, Arthur Andersen & Co. S.C., Center for Professional Education, St. Charles, Illinois.

Oliver W. Cummings is managing director of Shared Education Services, Arthur Andersen & Co. S.C., Center for Professional Education, St. Charles, Illinois.

A summative product evaluation is not as useful to a high-tech organization as is a formative evaluation that focuses on front-end process methodology and continual testing of the evolving product.

Evaluating and Ensuring High-Tech Product Quality

Edward S. Halpern

The most popular method of product evaluation is a product review that informs potential consumers about the worth of a given product. For example, *Consumer Reports* compares the merit, worth, and price of competing products, enabling buyers to make informed decisions about which product to purchase. Stereo magazines and computer magazines rate new equipment, critique new recordings, review PC software, and so on. Movie reviewers Siskel and Ebert's "thumbs up/thumbs down" assessment of movies is a simplistic example of a consumer-oriented review involving the opinion of the "expert." Such evaluations are summative.

From the perspective of an organization that develops and manufactures a product, a favorable review from any of the popular sources may stimulate product sales. When the product is not favorably reviewed, however, the organization must take action. If the product development cycle is several years long and making product changes is slow or costly, it may not be possible to make product modifications quickly enough or cheaply enough to attract or retain customers. This is often the case with high-tech products. To ensure market need, product quality, and customer satisfaction, a high-tech organization must conduct product evaluations at all stages of the product development cycle—from marketing and concept testing through field testing and customer review.

In large software products, the front-end capital investment may be enormous and the time span between identifying a product need and completing the product is lengthy. The cost of fixing a product error is enormous when compared with finding and fixing it during the early design stages. While estimates vary with the particular industry and method of measurement, the cost of fixing a software bug can be anywhere from ten to eighty times more if discovered by a customer than if discovered early in the design stages. This estimate does not include ill will on the part of the customer, who perceives an inadequate product—if the product survives at all. Just recently we have seen some failings in NASA's Hubble Space Telescope, and continuation of the project is now in jeopardy. Some industry experts wonder if running a simple yet critical test would have revealed and prevented the problem. The NASA development team must now ask what aspect of their development process permitted them to skip this test.

Product evaluation must occur at all stages of development, including, in order of occurrence, concept testing, prototype testing, requirements review, and unit, system, and field testing. These stages mark the developing product as it evolves from an idea, to a mockup, to a document, to a component, to multiple components, to the final product. The internal evaluator can guide the product evolution and development process by monitoring design and development activities relative to customer wants and needs. Data collection and feedback of results at planned intermediate stages can help to improve the product as well as the development process itself.

This chapter explores a product evaluation strategy for high-tech industries, with particular emphasis on software development. Specific examples regarding the design of the user interface are presented, since it is this that determines the customer's perception of quality.

Defining Product Quality

Commonly used definitions of product quality are "fitness for use" (Juran and Gryna, 1980), "an absence of defects," and "conformance to requirements" (Crosby, 1979). Product design requirements must state customer needs and define what is fit for use. The final product will be evaluated on whether the requirements accurately state customer needs and whether the product meets the stated requirements. Presumably, a presence of defects or a product that does not conform to requirements will not be fit for use (Quality Assurance Center, 1987).

Since most products have a variety of users or customers, what constitutes "fitness" will vary. In a large software development context, product stages are judged by "internal customers" because a product is developed by many different organizational groups in a lock-step sequence. Each intermediate deliverable will be judged as fit for use by each succeeding (or receiving) group. These deliverables define product stages and demand that some specific level of quality be achieved before development continues. At the front end, for example, a marketing organization defines a product or service that meets a customer or market need. A systems engineering organization takes that idea and writes detailed product requirements or specifications from the perspective of the customer—including how it should operate and how to handle user errors. These specifications are given to a software development organization that must approve them for comprehensibility, completeness, and feasibility. Any disagreement between organizational units must be resolved by clarification or negotiation. If some requirements cannot be met within the necessary time frame, there must be negotiations about how the requirements get changed. Features may get eliminated and user scenarios may need to be altered when the development group estimates costs and effort. Once the software is written, it is sent to the testing organization, where tests are run to ensure that the agreed-upon requirements are met and that the software is free of bugs.

Current quality programs in software development have adapted the techniques formerly used in manufacturing to monitor and control the software development process. Such monitoring is critical to the organization's and product's success because, as mentioned before, the earlier in the process errors or incorrect requirements are identified, the easier and less costly it is to make the desired changes.

Quality and Computer Technology. In discussing product quality in computer systems, we can look at the hardware, the software, and the human interface. The human interface addresses both hardware and software issues. The hardware refers to the physical parts of the computer—for example, the silicon chips, circuit boards, storage devices, keyboard, and monitor. The software refers to the programs, operating system, and applications. The human interface on the hardware side considers the ergonomics or physical design as it relates to human musculature, auditory and visual capabilities and limitations, and fatigue factors. The human interface on the software side considers variables of cognitive psychology, such as attention, memory, and ease of learning (Bailey, 1982). Most end users do not give much thought to these issues. They just want the product to work the way they think it should—and are critical whenever it does not.

When a manufacturer is automating the production of thousands of component parts or assembling complex products, machine imperfections may lead to unpredictable or defective results. Simply, there may be bad chips or loose screws. The evaluation system must be able to detect deficiencies before they are in the marketplace and to identify the process deficiencies that allowed the defective parts to be produced at all. For example, finding a loose screw is important. Finding the cause of the loose screw is more important.

A software product is largely controlled by people, the coordination of those people, and their tool support. It is not an automated process but, rather, a human process. As the software engineering discipline becomes more sophisticated for large projects, the emphasis on programming has moved from the individual to the engineering process (Humphrey, 1985). The goal is to create a product or set of services that is error-free and easy to use. The evaluation system must monitor the developing product to ensure that it conforms to valid specifications and to identify process bottlenecks.

In the early days, quality evaluations of hardware components involved inspections and quality control approaches. A software product poses different problems. There is nothing tangible to inspect. There are far too many scenarios, branches, and system states to test, and many are unanticipated. The emphasis must clearly be on the development process (Koono and Soga, 1990). Given a computer keyboard or a telephone, a user can press any key at any time. The system must not crash, lock out the user, or corrupt the data base, regardless of how unusual the user input is.

Testing the human factors quality of the physical design has become routine because many physical design guidelines are standardized. Recommendations exist for keyboard tilt, keypress depression tension, screen angle, and luminescence, and they may often be customized by the user. The physical product can be compared to the requirements specification fairly easily. On the software side, however, human interface design decisions vary considerably with the users' experience and their cognitive capabilities. The phenomenal number of software packages available and users' individual differences have made human interface design rife with issues that have an impact on customers' perceptions of quality. No longer is a bug-free product sufficient—the product must also have a good design and be easy to use (Koono and Soga, 1990).

Measuring Product Quality. A typical user-oriented product evaluation must measure both human and system performance. Variables include reliability and performance (consistency of operation, repair statistics, and response times), ease of use, user accuracy, and training time (Bailey, 1982). These factors are crucial to customer satisfaction. A typical evaluation focuses on the collection of such measures at each stage of the product development process and proposes modifications that will improve the evolving product (requirements to development; software module), as well as ways to make the process more efficient (getting earlier customer feedback; reporting problems quickly). High-tech companies normally have a formal methodology to guide the developing product. A professional evaluator can become involved at any stage or level.

By employing process quality management and improvement methods, along with formative product evaluation methods, evaluators can shape the evolving product as well as the underlying process for continual improvements. High-level evaluation questions must address issues of functionality, ease of use, and usability. Fundamental questions include:

• How can we ensure that the product or service offers the capabilities desired by the customer?

- How can we ensure that the product or service is easy to use?
- How can we ensure that the product is fast, reliable, and durable?
- How can we ensure that the product operations conform to the user's expectations and desires?

Ongoing Evaluation. Table 1 summarizes the various process and product quality methodologies that may guide the development of a software product for both formative and summative evaluations and for internal and external evaluations. The Product Evaluation column shows the use of tests at every stage of the product development cycle from concept testing to unit testing. The outcome of the product tests during summative evaluation indicates whether additional work is required or whether development may proceed to the next stage. The outcome of the product tests during the summative evaluation indicates customer perception, satisfaction, and product acceptance. There is continual interplay between assessing product quality at predefined stages and assessing process efficiency. The underlying theme is: If we have a substandard product (at any stage), how does our process need to be improved? Evaluators must be prepared to investigate both.

The Process Evaluation column indicates the methodologies that should be in place throughout the entire development process. Process quality management and improvement (PQMI), quality improvement programs (QIP), and quality audits are some of the formal methodologies for ensuring quality. The PQMI, which is both a philosophy and a methodology, supports a seven-step plan for implementing a corporate quality management system (AT&T Quality Steering Committee, 1987). These steps include assigning responsibilities, identifying customer requirements, defining metrics, assessing conformance to requirements, investigating the process to

Table 1. Product and Process Approaches to Quality

Focus	Product Evaluation	Process Evaluation
Formative		
Internal	Concept testing	PQMI, QIP, audits
	Simulation testing	
	Prototype testing	
	Requirements review	
	Unit testing	
External		Quality audits
Summative	Field testing	Quality audits
Internal	Usability testing	
External	Field testing	Quality audits
	Product comparisons	
	Usability testing	

identify improvement opportunities, ranking improvement opportunities and setting objectives, and improving process quality. Data are continually collected from users of the process in order to identify ways to make improvements. Process management tools include brainstorming, cause and effect analyses, customer needs analyses, interviews, surveys, and nominal group techniques, to name a few. Customer needs analyses help to define customer requirements. Brainstorming, cause and effect analyses, and interviews help the process team define metrics, assess conformance to customer requirements, and explore improvement opportunities. A process team leader facilitates process improvement teams in accord with the PQMI methodology. The leader must be familiar with the software development process, aware of the organizational interfaces, and skilled in running problem identification and conflict resolution sessions. The leader must be able to organize teams of people and stimulate the flow of ideas synergistically because ideas typically abound within the team but need to be channeled productively. These tasks are well matched to the action-oriented evaluator.

QIPs are comprised of groups of individuals assigned to specialized areas and responsible for planning and implementing quality improvements. They can be formed by any development work group that perceives process problems. The QIP investigates the problem and, if appropriate, recommends a solution. Having a leader with group facilitation skills is imperative to the success of the QIP.

Quality audits are done internally to oversee adherence to formal methodologies. Audits may also be done by external organizations acting on behalf of the customers, who want assurance that the quality methodologies directing development are being followed.

Evaluating Human Interfaces. In a technology-driven environment, it is easy to lose sight of the user-sensitive design issues; yet it is the users who will ultimately accept or reject the system. Thus it is imperative to build into the process features which assure that the final product will be easy for a user to operate. The goal of human factors or human interface work is "to optimize the performance of an entire system" (Day, 1989, p. 3). The system refers to a human and a machine working together. The human factors aspect of the system typically refers to the relationship between the system and user. A good user interface should be fast and convenient for experienced people and should be easy for the novice to learn (Draper and Norman, 1985).

Human factors issues relate to the cognitive characteristics of operators, such as their ability to perceive, remember, and reason. Design considerations include system feedback (tones, display messages), user input devices (mouse, keyboard, voice), user inputs (commands, menu choices), and user perception (auditory capabilities and limitations, visual capabilities and discriminations). When one is evaluating the user interface, data can be collected in a system laboratory with a simulation or prototype or in the field with a final product. The laboratory allows the investigator to develop user scenarios in a simulation or prototype and to collect objective data about user errors and system performance. In this environment, it is easy to manipulate conditions and to determine what users find as the simple operations, all before the requirements are finalized. Once in the field, user data are much more costly to obtain; moreover, they can only be collected with the customer's permission. As stated before, since these data are part of the completed product, it may be too costly to modify the design. Typical areas for inquiry include:

Is the System Easy to Use? People find products they love, but often they cannot use most of the options. This is true for VCRs, microwave ovens, CD players, cable TV, and telephones. The most critical items for an easy-to-use interface are: Is the interface obvious? Most users attempt to operate equipment without reading the (often cryptic) instruction manual. An obvious user interface does not require any effort, or at least it requires only minimal effort or expertise. Perceived ease of use can be assessed through interviews and surveys. Objective means can be obtained in the laboratory by logging user errors or, in the field, by analyzing keypress sequences. Is it consistent? Most users expect their system inputs and responses to be similar in all contexts. Consistency inspires user confidence in system operations. A consistent interface enables the user to generalize an operation to other features. Are the operations easy to remember? Users, particularly infrequent users, must be able to remember a few simple rules that work in many situations. Complex rules are not easily recalled when needed. Does the system provide helpful feedback? The system should respond to the user's inputs with an acknowledgment or confirmation. If there is an error, the feedback should be instructive. A message that reads "user error" rarely helps the user complete a task.

How Frequently Is the System Used? Frequency of use indicates both usefulness of a feature and ease of operation. This is important to telephone companies. People report that they do not use many telephone features because they cannot remember what access code works for which feature. Customers are often afraid to transfer a call lest they inadvertently disconnect the calling party. Perceived frequency of use can be estimated by surveying customers. Objective data may be obtained with the customer's permission through automated methods in which keypresses are stored in a data base for subsequent analysis.

Does It Perform Well? Users want systems that are responsive to their requests and are durable. Is the response time adequate? Users expect system responses to be quick and, more important, consistent. When response time varies, users may be confused about whether the system received their input. Actual response times can be measured with automated test equipment and analyzed for consistency. Acceptability can be gauged from surveys and interviews. *Is the system reliable?* Users want the system to work all of the time. When a system malfunctions, users find they cannot rely on it and will use it less frequently if at all. Trouble tickets and user logs can help the evaluator assess reliability. Again, interviews or surveys provide information about user acceptance of system failures.

Does the System Help Minimize Errors (Both Human and Machine)? Users should be prevented from making errors whenever possible. Through system prompts they can be guided as they proceed with tasks. An on-line help facility is also useful.

Does the User's Productivity Increase? In most business contexts, a large sum of money will be spent to update the telephones or provide better computer tools. Often the executive in charge will want some assurance that productivity will increase.

Is It Enjoyable to Use? When a system is enjoyable to operate, people will use it more often and be willing to spend more time learning new ways to use it. Good human factors design drives the customer's perception of product quality.

Product Design and Development

How can the user interface evaluation be integrated into the general software development methodology? As it concerns usability studies, product development may be divided into three broad phases: product definition, conformance testing, and user acceptance testing (see Figure 1). The product definition phase involves a detailed specification of how the product will work as well as ensuring that the product concept has a market and solves some business (or other user) problem. Conformance testing entails the assurance that the product functions as stated in the requirements and is free of bugs and faults. User acceptance testing is completed by customers with the finished product. The product must conform to users' expectations and be fit for use. This may entail allowing customers to test the system themselves, polling them after purchase, or using expert opinion. Figure 1 represents the stages in a high-tech product development cycle. The boxes under "Development" show the evolving product stages. The boxes under "Evaluation" show the testing activities that help determine whether the evolving product can progress to the next stage.

Marketing. Marketing inputs and specific customer requests start the ball rolling with some indication of a market need or customer problem. This is translated into a high-level definition of a set of product or service capabilities, cost constraints, and recommended completion dates.

Concept Definition. As part of the marketing phase, one or more conceptual models of a customer solution may be proposed. It might be represented as a set of visuals or a written proposal. It reflects input from

Figure 1. Parallel Development and Evaluation Functions

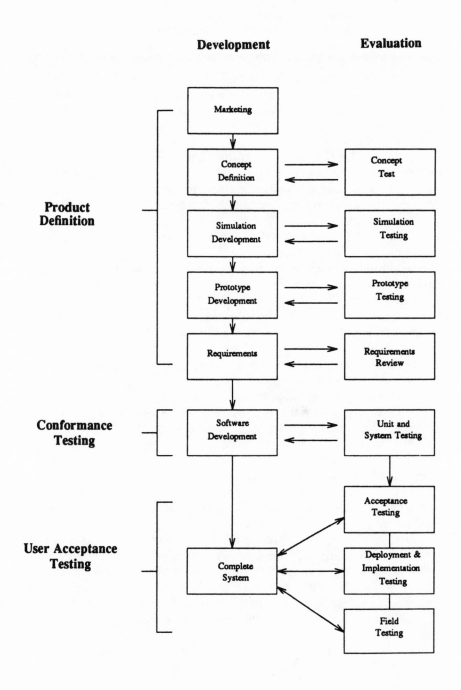

prospective users and knowledge about their environment. The concept should evolve with the help of customer feedback.

Concept Testing. The concept test is a tactic that can indicate whether the proposed product would solve a customer problem. Through visual representations, explanations, and dialogue with prospective users, the evaluator can investigate perceptions of the product's strengths and weaknesses, as well as the user's willingness to pay. The concept test also provides a mechanism for prospective users to contribute ideas to the final product definition. Without a clear and comprehensive indication of the capabilities at the front end, the finished product may not reflect customer needs or wishes.

Simulation Development. A simulation represents the item, equipment, operation, procedure, or environment (McCormick, 1976). It can be a single mockup of a piece of equipment or a sophisticated computer representation. Since it is a representation of a model, it has limited utility for prospective customer feedback.

Simulation Testing. A simulation provides the user with a concrete model of the product. Since the simulation looks and behaves like the proposed product, the user has a specific model or a number of alternative models to critique. A simulation is useful because it can be designed and developed quickly and is easy to modify. With one or more models, the various factors that contribute to ease of use can be tested and compared empirically. Prospective customers may be used as subjects to ensure a good user interface. Verbal protocols or think-aloud methods can help define an interface that conforms to user expectations (Hammond and others, 1987), as well as to indicate where users are likely to make errors in the proposed system. By videotaping users describing what they are doing with the system and why, the investigator is able to validate design assumptions and learn how inexperienced users operate the system.

Prototype Development. A prototype is a system model that looks and acts like the completed system (Benimoff and Whitten, 1989). It is helpful when formulating the feature requirements. From a user's view, it functions the same as a final product but does not have a full set of functions. The prototype is sufficient to solidify the concept and define a stable set of requirements.

Prototype Testing. The prototype allows users to have a hands-on experience with the product. It stimulates user input for ease of use and functionality. Not only can verbal protocols be obtained, but, in addition, users can try to complete multistage tasks in which the system responds and branches. Refinements to the product are still possible. User data that strongly suggest revisions will influence changes in the product requirements.

Requirements. Product requirements are the detailed written descriptions of the product, capabilities, and user interface.

Requirements Review. Developers must review the requirements for feasibility within the time, budget, and resource constraints. Any ambiguities must be clarified, development constraints must be clarified, and an accepted solution must be negotiated.

Software Development. The computer instructions that drive the hardware are written to provide the service. The code is the translation of the product design that can be compiled and executed to make the system work. The software must be reliable and conform to the product specifications.

Unit and System Testing. Unit tests are run on the software units to ensure that they work according to specification and are error-free. Test plans are written that reflect the requirements and are tested in the laboratory environment. System testing occurs when the units are combined together to ensure that the parts work together without errors.

Complete System. The complete system is the finished product that the customer owns or plans to purchase.

Acceptance Testing. Acceptance tests are optional and may be completed by the customer before accepting the product.

Deployment and Implementation Testing. When the product is deployed in the field, data may be collected on such issues as training effectiveness, learning time, smoothness of the transition, and support.

Field Testing. The testing in the field provides the last opportunity for the elimination of bugs. Minor feature enhancements may still be possible, but it is usually too late to make design changes. Software that does not conform to the requirements may be remedied somehow, but the product as it was conceptualized and defined must now stand on its own merits.

The Evaluator's Role

When undertaking a program evaluation, the outside evaluator is confronted with learning about the organization, program, stakeholders, politics, and policies. There is some flexibility in evaluation approaches because each situation brings new problems, personalities, and contexts. In a high-tech organization, the internal evaluator faces a formal project methodology that guides development. Normally the methodology conforms to generally accepted software development and testing procedures. Accepted procedures are those outlined by PQMI or a similar methodology. Evaluators may play a role as facilitators on the improvement teams and also define new areas where improvements can be made. Since the methodology is implemented by a large number of people, evaluating and improving the software development process requires an understanding of managing people.

There are product evaluation needs at every stage of the product development cycle. In the early stages of defining the product and formulating the requirements, the evaluator's role is to validate market needs and feasibility. Data may be collected through focus groups, interviews, or surveys. The evaluator must determine the prospective customer needs and the degree to which the proposed solution will solve those needs. The evaluator must also ensure that the market need perceived by the customer is the same need that appears in the product requirements. Often the evaluator can play a crucial role as an intermediary between the customer and engineer because the engineer typically builds the system and thus can lose sight of what it is like to operate it. The results of user studies can help development teams decide when it is worth the extra time to develop the product one way over another.

During simulation and prototype testing, the evaluator must collect more detailed data—first about whether the user will profit from the product and, second, whether the user can easily operate the system. Think-aloud protocols may supply information about what users expect from the system and why (Kato, 1986). Experimentally controlled task completion tests supply objective data about users' ability to operate the system (McCormick, 1976), what situations cause them to make errors, and what kind of training will be required.

During development and testing, the evaluator is concerned with whether the requirements represent a comprehensive product description and then whether the software is error-free (Pettijohn, 1986). The requirements review is a forum to identify missing or inconsistent information or lack of conformance to conclusions from previous stages. Unit and system testing require testing scenarios for errors and, if necessary, revising the code. This is not an evaluator's job. Testing is typically left to the development teams.

During deployment, the evaluator is concerned with the transition from the old system to the new. The evaluator may determine whether there was adequate training and find out how users respond to the changes. During the field testing, the evaluator must determine the overall impact of the product and learn about the customer's attitudes and utilization of the product. A full gamut of evaluation activities may be attempted, ranging from a field experiment to a field study. Data may be collected via interviews, surveys, observations, trouble reports, and daily logs. Detailed objective data may be collected by trapping and time stamping every interaction between user and system and then analyzing them for feature use, user errors, and system response times. As with any evaluation project, the data collection needs will vary with the product and the organization commissioning the evaluation.

Summary and Conclusion

Evaluation activities should occur at all stages of the product's life cycle—from conceptualization to field testing. The internal evaluator may collect and analyze data at each stage in the product's evolution, as well as data about the processes designed to ensure quality. Special attention should be given to the human factors or usability factors of a high-tech product. When the user interface is evaluated very early in the design process, modifications can be made to reflect users' expectations, thereby ensuring their overall satisfaction when the product is used in the field.

References

AT&T Quality Steering Committee. *Process Quality Management and Improvement Guidelines*. Indianapolis, Ind.: Publication Center, AT&T Bell Laboratories, 1987.

Bailey, R. W. *Human Performance Engineering: A Guide for System Designers*. Englewood Cliffs, N.J.: Prentice-Hall, 1982.

Benimoff, N. I., and Whitten, W. B., II. "Human Factors Approaches to Prototyping and Evaluating User Interfaces." *AT&T Technical Journal*, 1989, 68, 44–55.

Crosby, P. B. *Quality Is Free: The Art of Making Quality Certain*. New York: McGraw-Hill, 1979.

Davis, B. "After Recent Setbacks, NASA Faces a Fight over Project Funding." *Wall Street Journal*, July 9, 1990, p. 1.

Day, M. C. "Designing the Human Interface: An Overview." *AT&T Technical Journal*, 1989, 68, 2–8.

Draper, S. W., and Norman, D. A. "Software Engineering for User Interfaces." *IEEE Transactions in Software Engineering*, 1985, SE-11, 252–258.

Hammond, K., and others. "The Role of Cognitive Psychology in User-Interface Design." In M. Gardiner and B. Christie (eds.), *Applying Cognitive Psychology to User-Interface Design*. New York: Wiley, 1987.

Humphrey, W. S. "The IBM Large-System Software Development Process: Objectives and Directions." *IBM Systems Journal*, 1985, 24, 76–78.

Juran, J. M., and Gryna, F. M., Jr. *Quality Planning and Analysis: From Product Development Through Use*. New York: McGraw-Hill, 1980.

Kato, T. "What Question-Asking Protocols Can Say About the User Interface." *International Journal of Man-Machine Studies*, 1986, 25, 659–673.

Koono, Z., and Soga, M. "Structural Ways of Thinking as Applied to Quality Assurance Management." *IEEE Journal on Selected Areas in Communications*, 1990, 8, 291–300.

McCormick, E. J. *Human Factors in Engineering and Design*. New York: McGraw-Hill, 1976.

Pettijohn, C. L. "Achieving Quality in the Development Process." *AT&T Technical Journal*, 1986, 65, 85–93.

Quality Assurance Center. *Quality by Design*. Indianapolis, Ind.: Publication Center, AT&T Bell Laboratories, 1987.

Edward S. Halpern is a member of technical staff at AT&T Bell Laboratories in the Switching Services and Customer Applications Planning Department, where he is responsible for designing and evaluating human interfaces for new products.

Academic efforts in evaluation and research have contributed to focus-group methodology, thereby helping business and industry to use focus groups for more than marketing research.

Focus-Group Interviewing: New Strategies for Business and Industry

Richard A. Krueger

Focus groups began in the public sector, received early attention by social scientists, and then languished into disuse in the academic community. Focus-group methodology did not flourish in the public or academic environment but rather in American business and industry. Only in the past decade has focus-group interviewing been rediscovered by the academic community. During the past five decades of focus-group evolution, both the business and academic sectors have contributed to its development—each responding to differing environments and values. This chapter examines the development of focus-group interviewing and offers suggestions for use beyond marketing research.

During the late 1930s social scientists were investigating the values of nondirective individual interviewing. Doubts had been raised about the accuracy of information gathered by traditional methods such as one-to-one interviews and mail-out surveys. Survey results were not consistent with observed behavior, and the interviewer's influence on the respondent in one-to-one interviews was in question. The limitations of predetermined, close-ended questions often used in both individual interviews and mail-out surveys were becoming apparent. The traditional interview with predetermined response categories had a major disadvantage: Since the respondent was limited by the choices offered, the findings were constrained by the oversight or omission of the interviewer. By contrast, the nondirective procedures, which incorporated open-ended questions, began with limited assumptions and placed considerable emphasis on getting in touch with

NEW DIRECTIONS FOR PROGRAM EVALUATION, no. 49, Spring 1991 ©Jossey-Bass Inc., Publishers the reality of the interviewee. Social scientists began emphasizing a different role for researchers—one that would be less directive and dominating. In this new role the emphasis was on a nondirective interview that would allow the respondent to comment on the areas he or she deemed most important.

The nondirective interview using open-ended questions gained popularity and was increasingly used by social scientists and psychologists in the late 1930s and 1940s. Roethlisberger and Dickson (1938) cited it in studies of employee motivation, and Carl Rogers (1942) used it in psychotherapy. A major contribution to the field of interviewing occurred during World War II when the U.S. government commissioned sociologist Robert Merton and his colleagues to examine military morale. Many of the procedures that have come to be accepted as common practice in focus-group interviews were based on that research and set forth in the classic work by Merton, Marjorie Fiske, and Patricia L. Kendall, *The Focused Interview* (1956).

Public-Sector Eclipse, Private-Sector Discovery

Focus-group interviewing in the academic sector began an eclipse shortly after World War II that was to last almost three decades. Social scientists had a number of reasons for maintaining some distance from focus-group interviews. There was a tendency to be preoccupied with quantitative procedures and assume that reality could be determined a priori. Interpreting the interactive effects of a group's discussion, dealing with inconsistent comments, determining how to make sense of information when one group member influenced others—all presented problems for the prevailing positivistic paradigm. The evolution of focus groups (and for that matter qualitative research methods in general within the academic community) took a subordinate position for decades to come. As recently as 1985, not one of the nation's top twenty-five graduate business schools offered courses in qualitative research techniques (Hollander and Oromaner, 1986). Rather, graduate business schools emphasized statistical methodology. After all, statistical procedures were familiar to graduate faculty, they were readily teachable, and students' abilities could be easily measured. By contrast, students had to acquire qualitative experience either from practicing masters in the field or from other academic departments such as psychology, sociology, education, or anthropology.

Focus-group interviewing gained early respectability in business and industry because of its high face validity and practical applications. Early uses in business and industry were primarily in marketing research, where the goal was to discover more about consumer behavior in order to increase sales. The outcome measure was specific: increased profitability. By the mid-1950s American business and industry were discovering the importance of consumer perceptions. The prevailing emphasis in American business up until then had been on sales. This was the country that institutionalized the traveling salesman—and if your product wasn't selling, the solution was to replace the sales force with new people. By the mid-1950s the pent-up consumer demand from World War II had been met and many new companies were aggressively competing for the consumer's dollar. In addition, the public was becoming increasingly concerned about the concepts of quality, service, and value. The business that could stay in tune with the consumer could achieve a larger share of the market.

Marketing research began as a smart investment to get the jump on the competition, and over the past forty years it has expanded and flourished. Successful businesses discovered the importance of determining public wants and then advertising products using messages that were meaningful to potential customers. Focus-group interviews filled a niche by enabling business and industry to understand customer thinking. In fact, focus-group interviewing thrived in business and industry in the 1960s and 1970s. Results were used in advertising campaigns centered on what the consumer considered to be the positive attributes of the product. Soft drink companies, for example, discovered via focus groups that consumers drink beverages not because of thirst but because of the sociability associated with the product. It is no wonder, then, that slogans promoting these beverages highlight how "things go better" or increase one's personal popularity on the beach (Bellenger, Bernhardt, and Goldstucker, 1976).

Focus groups have proved useful outside the world of advertising, as well. There are numerous examples. The Pillsbury Company used focus groups in 1976 to obtain consumers' reaction to frozen pizza. The most enlightening discovery coming out of the focus groups was their intense dissatisfaction with the crust. Consumers said it tasted like cardboard. This insight sparked Pillsbury researchers to develop their very successful Totino's Crisp Crust Frozen Pizza (Ingrassia, 1980). In the late 1970s, General Electric was tied for fourth place in microwave sales. Then focus groups identified a common lament of owners—microwave ovens take up valuable counter space. Shortly after this discovery, GE introduced an over-the-range microwave and called it the "Spacemaker." The new product was coupled with an advertising strategy which implied that the owner would gain additional kitchen space (Antilla and Sender, 1982). A movie studio that had received numerous awards and quintupled profits in five years regularly used focus groups to test audience reactions to possible endings for new films (Vichas, 1983). A firm that had considered manufacturing air conditioning filters for automobiles abandoned the idea after conducting focus groups. Customers just did not see the need for the filter, would not pay the price, and worried about how it would affect the car's air conditioner. The small investment in focus groups saved the company from making a very costly and unprofitable investment in a new product (Cox,

Higginbotham, and Burton, 1976). In short, focus-group interviews have become widely accepted in business and industry because they produce believable results at a reasonable cost.

New Interest from the Academic Sector

The pragmatic focus-group results produced by business and industry did not go unnoticed in the academic community. Academic researchers were struggling with the complexity of human decision making and troubled by the inadequacy of survey research procedures. Not only did the focus-group interview offer a means of gaining insight into human behavior, but the academic community also sought to improve on aspects of the focus-group interview.

The greatest academic contribution to focus-group methodology was in qualitative data analysis. Quality of analysis has been a problem of focus groups in the business community. Indeed, in many cases there just was no analysis, only a listing of participants' comments. Edwin Sonnecken (1986), former vice-president with Goodyear Tire & Rubber Company, describes the type of focus-group analysis often delivered by research agencies: "The report is usually turned over verbatim to the client. Sometimes the tape recordings or video recordings are useful. If the client desires, a research company may provide an interpretation of the interview findings, but this is not invariably true" (p. 43). Focus-group professionals were reluctant to undertake the interpretative analysis for several reasons: It takes time, it requires considerably more expertise and background knowledge than just presenting the verbatim comments, and, finally, the interpretative approach has an aura of subjectivity.

Scholars in the social sciences have been working intensively on qualitative data analysis for three decades and have made major contributions to the field. Foremost in this effort have been Glaser and Strauss (1967), Glaser (1978), Strauss (1987), Patton (1990), Taylor and Bogdan (1984), Miles and Huberman (1984), and Tesch (1990). Systematic and verifiable procedures have been established that remove much of the subjectivity from the analysis process. A number of procedures have been introduced to foster quality control of analysis: the systematic use of transcripts, adherence to accepted analysis protocol, computer text management and analysis, use of assistant moderators for increased objectivity, and focus-group audits to ensure adherence to overall procedures.

The academic environment values open access to information and collegial or peer review. As a result, most academic focus-group reports are available and subject to feedback from other academics. The traditional academic values of quality control coupled with availability of focus-group reports has resulted in procedures that improve the methodology. Standards have begun to emerge with respect to recruitment and sampling, the number of focus groups, the discussion environment, and the skills of the moderating team.

New Opportunities in Business and Industry

In the decades ahead it is likely that focus groups will continue to be widely used in marketing research, but other uses will continue to emerge in organizational development, training, customer relations, and employee benefits. The following paragraphs suggest some of the possibilities.

Developing Strategic Plans. Focus-group interviewing has been beneficial to organizations in the development of strategic plans. Successful strategic planning often includes a variety of data sources, and the focus-group interview offers several unique benefits. It has the potential for obtaining detailed alternative views, for discovering the rationale behind those points of view, and for involving people in a process where they are listened to and not lectured on the values of the current organizational position. Both the results and the process are proving beneficial to organizations.

At the University of Wisconsin, for example, focus-group interviews were effective in developing the strategic plan for the university's Cooperative Extension Service. By systematically listening to community leaders, to residents who have used agency resources, and to potential users of university resources, the university's decision makers were able to target their outreach efforts more effectively. The research team assumed that the university was the primary source of information on such topics as agriculture, home economics, community development, and youth development. Researchers were surprised at the number of resources that residents were currently using—they could identify a host of information sources. One of the positive side-effects was the enhanced esteem that focus-group participants had for the university after being invited to participate in the process (Sadowske, 1988).

The Minnesota Department of Education conducted thirty-two focus-group interviews in an effort to develop plans and legislative requests relating to emotionally and behaviorally disturbed students in public schools. Through focus groups with teachers, school administrators, social service and human service professionals, school support staff, parents, and students the research team was able to identify a common set of needs that cut across all groups. These needs included early intervention procedures, increased attention to interagency cooperation, greater parental involvement, and better training of educators.

Identifying Employee Training Needs. Good training is expensive; bad training costs even more. Focus groups can be used for exploring the relationships between people and topics that are critical to success. In some situations the environment and interrelationships are as important as the topic of training. Consider the following example.

The U.S. Department of Agriculture is currently facing a problem with water quality. Many of the practices that make American agriculture profitable have been causing environmental problems. One area of concern is the use of chemicals that can contaminate groundwater. The Extension Service has the potential to mobilize a nationwide staff effort to address this problem. In preparation for wide-scale action, the department sought to determine the training needs of county extension agents and university specialists around the nation—the key people who would conduct future educational efforts. Focus-group interviews were conducted in nineteen locations around the country. One of the valuable discoveries that emerged from the focus groups was that county agents are not in universal agreement that water quality is a top priority in their work schedules. In the decentralized extension system, considerable programming emphasis has been placed on grass-roots input and local residents have often been indifferent about water quality. County agents receive many requests for their time and use several practical strategies for determining priority. Since administrators regularly send new messages signaling what is important, agents have learned to be cautious of literal adherence to administrative advice. Agents indicated that they use three criteria to determine the importance of a new topic for the organization. New money is invested in the problem; new staff members are assigned to the program; and administrators regularly talk about the new problem. County agents indicated that these criteria would also influence their allocation of time to water quality (Casey, Krueger, and Bergsrud, 1989).

Identifying Concerns in Worker Relations. In some situations organizations need to make extra efforts in obtaining insights and comments from employees. Concerns can fester and grow out of proportion despite the best efforts of employee-relation professionals. Focus groups can provide a systematic way to get in touch with employees' concerns or test potential solutions.

Robin Bischoff (1989), for example, suggests that "employee listening" can be beneficial in developing a company benefits program. Careful listening procedures can help to eliminate employees' suspicion about flexible benefit plans. Bischoff suggests both a quantitative approach using paper and pencil and a qualitative strategy with individual interviews or small focus groups.

In a position paper from Catalyst's Corporate Child Care Resource, focus-group interviews were used to assess employees' need for child-care services. The focus group helped the employer learn more about the extent and urgency of employees' needs for affordable child care. The employer felt it had received valuable guidance from employees' experiences and has been able to develop a more effective corporate policy on child care (*Focus Groups*, 1983).

Identifying Problems and Solutions. Care must be exercised in identifying a problem and solution strategies. Sometimes the solutions need to be tested; at other times the problem is incorrectly diagnosed. The University of Minnesota's College of Agriculture, for example, was concerned about its declining enrollment of rural youth. High school graduates from small rural Minnesota schools were enrolling in agricultural colleges in neighboring states. Administrators assumed that this trend was caused by high school counselors who were either unfamiliar with the university or overly zealous in their support of other schools. A series of focus groups with potential students revealed that the problem was incorrectly diagnosed. The young people themselves had some negative notions about the university, and, in fact, the university was unwittingly adding to their erroneous perceptions. Students from small rural high schools saw the University of Minnesota as too big and impersonal. They felt they would get lost in the thousands of students and therefore preferred smaller schools. With this insight, the faculty took another look at the promotional materials being distributed to prospective students. The descriptive brochures had numerous photos of the university—pictures of the campus mall with thousands of students and pictures showing the grandeur of the university. The brochures told of the millions of books in the library, the thousands of students in the university, and the scores and scores of departments and majors. Clearly these promotional materials reinforced the fears of potential students. As a result of focus-group research, faculty members designed a special brochure that emphasized the "more compact" St. Paul campus, "friendly teachers who take an interest in you," and the benefits of attending college with other students from rural communities (Casey, 1987).

Developing Quality Control Procedures. Quality can be difficult to define for a variety of reasons: multiple interpretations, the recent history of the organization, and the values of executives, to name a few. Focus-group interviews can be helpful in obtaining the customer's perspective of quality—a perspective that may differ from that of company employees, whether they be executives, engineers, or sales personnel. Consider these two examples.

Mercy Hospital and Medical Center, a San Diego medical facility, was concerned about quality control procedures in patients' billing practices and patient relations. After conducting five focus groups with former patients, the researchers uncovered several aspects of the billing process that met with patients' disfavor. The study led to changes in the billing procedures that have recently met with positive response from patients (Bernstein, Harris, and Meloy, 1989).

At Fidelity Investor Information Services, focus groups coupled with telephone and written surveys proved helpful in maintaining quality services to customers. After listening to customers Fidelity responded with an 800 number, changes in financial statements, adoption of a client inquiry tracking system, and additional training for field employees ("How Can You Improve Service?," 1988).

Conclusion

Focus-group interviewing has become a multimillion-dollar industry in America and the principal method for conducting qualitative marketing research, largely because of the contributions of business and industry. The early adoption in business and industry occurred because the technique works—not because it met the accepted standards of academic rigor. Furthermore, it worked well enough to give business decision makers confidence to adopt or drop new products and develop marketing strategies. By contrast, the research community is less market driven and has had little incentive to "get the jump" on the competition. Nevertheless, professionals in business can benefit from development and refinements in the research community. The academic traditions of open access to information and rigorous collegial review have enhanced quality control. This improvement has occurred through developments in qualitative data analysis as well as adoption of systematic focus-group procedures. While the business community has led the way in achieving practicality, the academic community has improved on the procedures for application. With the contributions that have emerged from the academic research community, today American business and industry can obtain valuable information by making greater use of focus-group interviewing.

References

Antilla, S., and Sender, H. "Getting Customers in Focus." *Duns Business Month*, 1982, *119* (5), 73–80.

Bellenger, D. N., Bernhardt, K. L., and Goldstucker, J. L. *Qualitative Research in Marketing*. Chicago: American Marketing Association, 1976.

Bernstein, L., Harris, J., and Meloy, R. "Focus Groups Improve Billing Practices, Patient Relations." *Healthcare Financial Management*, 1989, *45* (5), 57–60.

Bischoff, R. N. "Lending an Ear to Employees' Benefits Needs." *Management World*, 1989, *18* (2), 24–26.

Casey, M. A. "Marketing Agricultural Education." Paper presented at Agricultural Education Central States Research Conference, Chicago, February 1987.

Casey, M. A., Krueger, R. A., and Bergsrud, F. *National Assessment of Water Quality Training Needs for Cooperative Extension Staff*. St. Paul: Minnesota Extension Service, 1989.

Cox, K. C., Higginbotham, J. B., and Burton, J. "Applications of Focus Group Interviews in Marketing." *Journal of Marketing*, 1976, *409* (1), 77–80.

Focus Groups: A Needs Assessment Approach to Corporate Child Care Policy Planning. New York: Catalyst, 1983.

Glaser, B. G. *Theoretical Sensitivity*. Mill Valley, Calif.: Sociology Press, 1978.

Glaser, B. G., and Strauss, A. L. *The Discovery of Grounded Theory: Strategies for Qualitative Research*. Hawthorne, N.Y.: Aldine, 1967.

Hollander, S. L., and Oromaner, D. S. "Seminars Fill Gap in Focus-Group Training." *Marketing News*, 1986, *20* (1), 1.

"How Can You Improve Service? Ask Your Customers—That's What Fidelity Did." *MarketFacts*, 1988, *7* (4), 17–18.

Ingrassia, L. "A Matter of Taste: There's No Way to Tell If a New Food Product Will Please the Public." *Wall Street Journal*, February 1980, pp. 1–23.

Krueger, R. A. *Focus Groups: A Practical Guide for Applied Research.* Newbury Park, Calif.: Sage, 1988.

Merton, R. K., Fiske, M., and Kendall, P. L. *The Focused Interview.* New York: Free Press, 1956.

Miles, M. B., and Huberman, M. A. *Qualitative Data Analysis: A Sourcebook of New Methods.* Newbury Park, Calif.: Sage, 1984.

Morgan, D. L. *Focus Groups as Qualitative Research.* Newbury Park, Calif.: Sage, 1988.

Patton, M. Q. *Qualitative Evaluation and Research Methods.* (2nd ed.) Newbury Park, Calif.: Sage, 1990.

Roethlisberger, F. J., and Dickson, W. J. *Management and the Worker.* Cambridge, Mass.: Harvard University Press, 1938.

Rogers, C. R. *Counseling and Psychotherapy.* Boston: Houghton Mifflin, 1942.

Sadowske, S. "Focus Groups for State Strategic Planning: Overview and Assessment." Paper presented at the American Evaluation Association, New Orleans, October 27, 1988.

Sonnecken, E. H. "When and How to Use Marketing Research Agencies." In V. Buell (ed.), *Handbook of Modern Marketing.* New York: McGraw-Hill, 1986.

Strauss, A. L. *Qualitative Analysis for Social Scientists.* New York: Cambridge University Press, 1987.

Taylor, S. J., and Bogdan, R. *Introduction to Qualitative Research Methods.* (2nd ed.) New York: Wiley, 1984.

Tesch, R. *Qualitative Research: Analysis Types and Software Tools.* New York: Falmer Press, 1990.

Vichas, R. P. "Eleven Ways Focus Groups Produce Profit-Making Ideas." *Marketing Times,* 1983, *30* (2), 17–18.

Richard A. Krueger is a professor and evaluation leader with the Minnesota Extension Service at the University of Minnesota, St. Paul. He is also adjunct professor in the Department of Vocational and Technical Education at the University of Minnesota.

The sociotechnical framework of organizational activity and relations should be explored as a preferable alternative to the rational framework as a context from which to design and conduct evaluations in business and industry.

Sociotechnical Theory: An Alternative Framework for Evaluation

Joanne Farley

The purpose of this volume is to explore how the theory and practice of evaluation may contribute to the needs of business and industry. This chapter presumes that evaluation must be conducted within some theoretical context that structures the relations between the subject of the evaluation and the role of evaluative inquiry. This chapter, therefore, explores the differences in the role defined for evaluation in two alternative models of organizational research and practice: the rational framework and the sociotechnical framework.

A second assumption is that although the rational framework has dominated corporate thought for the last century and a half, current philosophical, political, social, and economic trends are rendering this framework inadequate or even obsolete. Indeed, the increasing inconsistency between the rational framework and post–World War II realities may be forcing a paradigmatic revolution such as that described by Yvonna Lincoln (1985) in organizational research and practice. To the extent that this is true, evaluation must reconsider the theoretical contexts that structure its relations to corporate entities and corporate audiences. This chapter offers a focus for such a reconsideration.

The Rational Framework

Charles Taylor (1974) has observed that at the heart of every social theory is some conception of an agenda of human needs or desires that provides the theory with its explanatory force. The two organizational frameworks discussed here are no exception. The rational model rests on a principle of psychological motivation that has served as the basis for liberal political theory since the seventeenth century. This principle states that human beings are primarily motivated by the self-interested goal of satisfying their needs and wants and avoiding those events, conditions, or objects which cause them discomfort or displeasure. Moreover, Anthony Downs (1957) notes that while goal orientation is one hallmark of the modern definition of rationality, the second is efficiency. He observes that "the term *rational* is never applied to an agent's ends, but only to his means. This follows from the definition of rational as efficient, i.e., maximizing output for a given input, or minimizing input for a given output" (p. 5).

The concept of the rational actor derives from the abstraction of humans existing in a state of nature, devoid of the rule of law or politics. In this state of nature, humans are essentially atomistic as well as individual-istic. Social consciousness emerges only with the realization that other individuals represent a constraint on (or threat to) the individual's ability to attain goals or that social cooperation will result in greater gain than could be had by the efforts of a single individual. Interests external to the individual are relevant only insofar as they must be dealt with in the pursuit of goals.

The rational framework, then, characterizes the individual as atomistic, individualistic, self-interested, goal-oriented, and rational or efficient. It is essential to understand the relations between these characteristics since they lead to a particular conceptualization of human nature that is repeatedly mirrored and extended to yield a characterization of the rational organization. This characterization encompasses a view of the organization's internal composition, its relation to its environment, and the structuring of human relations within the organization. While space does not permit a full discussion of these extensions, a brief overview is offered here.

Like the individual in the state of nature, the organization is atomistic and individualistic in that it establishes its goals by reference to self-interest (as defined by management) and strategically pursues them as rationally as possible. Internally, the organization is composed of separate and distinct units and subunits, each of which has specialized tasks to perform. The organization is hierarchical: Authority flows from the upper levels of management downward through the organization. There is thus a sharp demarcation between management and labor and a correspondingly clear distinction between decision making and implementation. Labor is seen as one of several factors of production, and its deployment is based on calculations regarding the mix of factors that will most efficiently move the organization toward its goals. The environment in which the organization operates can likewise be separated into discrete entities that are relevant only to the extent they impede or facilitate the pursuit of the organization's goals.

Before turning to the role of evaluation, we must briefly consider the relation between science and the rational framework. The predominant paradigm for the conduct of natural and social science emerged from the same theories that provided us with the notion of the rational actor. The trademarks of this paradigm—its atomistic and deterministic view of reality—reflect the birthright it shares with the rational model. Indeed, science has been hailed as the epitome of "rational" knowledge due to its success in explaining how causal factors combine to produce certain outcomes. The cause-effect orientation of science serves as a natural bridge to the means-end orientation of the rational organization.

Over the last two centuries, the scientific community has made breakthroughs in knowledge that have resulted in technologies which greatly enhance industrial productivity and efficiency. Thus business and industry have increasingly become the sponsors of scientific research that generates knowledge used to produce goods and services more efficiently as well as to produce new types of goods and services. The use of scientific knowledge has not been limited to production processes. As Clark (1985) points out, social scientific research has also resulted in human technologies that supposedly enhance the efficiency of management systems. Examples include new management information systems, program planning and budgeting systems, futures studies, and marketing and needs assessment techniques.

In discussing the relationship between the liberal concept of rationality and social science, Hans Peter Dreitzel (1974) observes: "Technological as well as social scientific knowledge can only be used if mediated and transformed by a group of experts who understand this kind of knowledge and can adjust it to the strategic needs of those using it: the state and the corporations" (p. 365). Dreitzel describes four ways in which the technocrat may relate to his or her sponsor: as an expert on the application of technology; as an expert on expediency who analyzes the compatibility of different means with different goals; as an expert on strategies who is concerned with organizational procedures, political forces, and strategies of persuasion beyond means and ends; and as an expert on the technical rationality of the goals themselves—that is, examining whether a certain goal is, in fact, in the long-term interests of the firm.

Dreitzel's account of the possible roles of the technocrat is applicable to the evaluator in the rational firm. The applicability is exemplified in an article written by Calingo, Perloff, and Bryant for the 1984 *Evaluation Studies Review Annual*. In this article, the authors outline three primary management functions that represent targets of opportunity for evaluation practice. First is the strategic level at which managers are concerned with identifying those strategies that will best enable the organization to deal with the external environment. Evaluation at the strategic level focuses on identifying those markets and products in which the firm can most successfully compete and determining the strategies that will result in successful competition.

The second, or coordinative, level is concerned with ensuring that the internal structure and operations of the organization enable it to effectively implement the decisions emanating from the strategic level. Coordinative evaluation focuses on outcome monitoring to determine whether internal processes are producing the desired and anticipated level of outcomes at the right time. Coordinative evaluation also encompasses summative evaluation including impact and cost-benefit assessments of the performance of internal programs and activities.

The third and last management level is the operational function, which deals with the "efficient and effective execution of organizational tasks" (p. 717). Evaluation at this level is primarily formative and assesses the extent to which organizational tasks are carried out as planned and with the expected degree of efficiency. In doing so, operational evaluation also seeks to identify where internal processes may be improved.

While the rational framework has predominated in organizational research since at least the mid-nineteenth century, researchers are increasingly questioning its adequacy in explaining or prescribing organizational behavior. These criticisms have significant implications for evaluation conducted within the rational framework. Several of these concerns merit discussion.

First, critics suggest that the rational framework's explanatory and prescriptive assumptions are no longer consistent with the realities of corporate dynamics or the environment in which they must operate. The postwar world has seen major transformations as new economic superpowers have emerged and national markets once closed to American business have now opened. Moreover, political, social, and economic interdependency has increased as national boundaries have become more permeable and indistinct. This interdependency has resulted in an international economy that is constantly in a state of flux. New developments, problems, or crises in one sector create ripples throughout the whole so that no participant is insulated from the effects. As a result, financial, international, technological, and consumer markets have become vastly more complex and subject to change. This trend looks likely to increase rather than decrease as more players join the international economy and national economies become ever more interlocked (Morgan, 1986).

Critics say that in the face of the increasing interdependence and instability of the international economy, the rational framework can no longer sustain its atomistic, mechanistic, and individualistic approach to the relation between organization and environment. Moreover, firms organized on rationalist principles are characterized by functional hierarchy, compartmentalization, specialization, and calculability (Clark, 1985). These characteristics reinforce rigidity of thought and action. Yet corporations must now move quickly and flexibly to find creative solutions to the new problems generated by the instability and complexity of the economic environment. This need gives rise, in turn, to a need for new ways of conceptualizing the internal relations of organizational components (Peters and Waterman, 1982; Argyris, 1982).

Critics also claim that the rationalist explanation of organizational planning and goal setting is frequently inaccurate. As a rational actor, the corporation is viewed as a fairly simple entity whose behavior is a direct consequence of decisions made by management, which acts single-mindedly and with unanimity of purpose in pursuing the goals it specifies for the organization. In many cases, however, corporations are actually composed of numerous groups competing internally to direct the course of the organization. From this pluralist view, organizational behavior must be explained as an outcome of the political interplay of power and influence wielded by these internal factions. The need for compromise that results from pluralistic decision-making contexts often results in a "muddling through" approach to planning and in the emergence of inconsistent goals and objectives. The notion of organizational activity being determined by the sometimes muddled directions posed by compromise stands in stark contrast to the exacting standards for decision making required by the rational framework (Morgan, 1986).

Rationalist evaluators may protest that the muddledness of pluralistic decisions confirms the appropriateness of the rational model as a prescriptive guide for organizational behavior. However, a number of researchers (Patterson, Purkey, and Parker, 1986; Weick, 1976) suggest that pluralism may be the natural state of many organizations rather than an aberration. If this is true, evaluators looking for the clear goals posited by the rational model will be searching for a will-o'-the-wisp and, consequently, will have little of value to say to the organizations they serve. Moreover, as discussed later, other scholars argue that beyond being a fact of organizational life, pluralism is a necessary and desirable characteristic enabling corporations to operate effectively in the postwar environment.

The management orientation of the rational framework is problematic for evaluation in other ways. Calingo, Perloff, and Bryant point out that "since management is the ultimate sponsor and user of such evaluations, these evaluation opportunities need to be defined within the context of the management function in industry" (1984, p. 716). However, a number of evaluation theorists argue that it is unfair to evaluate activities involving numerous stakeholder groups from the perspective of one single group (Weiss, 1983). Other critics point out that groups which have no stake in the evaluation or its results are less likely to be committed to using its recommendations.

There are other significant problems with the rational framework as a context from which to conduct evaluation. These problems relate to its logical and normative adequacy. First, rationalist evaluation is limited to a purely instrumental or technical activity. Carl Hempel (1965) makes the distinction between "relative" or "instrumental" judgments on the one hand and "absolute" or "categorical" judgments on the other. Scientific methods can provide us with a basis for making only statements of the former type—such as, for example, the claim that "Given goal G, action A based on scientific evidence is a more efficient means for achieving G than alternative action B." However, the absolute or categorical judgment that action A is therefore "good" cannot be derived from scientific knowledge since it is empirically neither confirmable nor disconfirmable. Hempel's argument is applied to rationalist evaluation as well as to scientific research insofar as the presumed aim of evaluation is to produce instrumental and neutral knowledge.

However, the presumed neutrality of rationalist evaluation may not be logically or practically possible. Charles Taylor convincingly argues that the explanation of nontrivial findings about human or political phenomena cannot be value-free: "A given explanatory framework secretes a notion of good, and a set of valuations, which cannot be done away with—though they can be overridden—unless we do away with the framework" (1974, p. 169). Thus, for example, the finding that a particular staff training program has increased participants' expertise in certain skill areas derives its significance from the theoretical relations established in the rational framework between specialized skills (expertise), productivity, and efficiency. Moreover, because productivity and efficiency are central to fulfillment of the rational actor's needs (the fulfillment of self-interested goals), the finding entails a positive normative valuation of the staff training in question. In short, the finding is intelligible only because of its derivation from the rational framework in which a positive valuation is a priori attached to productivity and efficiency. Thus the evaluator cannot escape normative implications so long as he or she relies on a theoretical framework that explains human motivation, activity, or organization.

A related criticism charges that in allowing their activities to be defined in atomistic, instrumental, and neutral terms, rationalist evaluators allow organizational stakeholders to ignore the social role played by the firm. Yet this perspective is irresponsible in the face of increasing evidence that while businesses may be private organizations, their actions have very public consequences. We are daily learning more about how the technologies employed by business and industry are polluting our natural environment, how their marketing campaigns may be resulting in unhealthy consumer responses (for example, encouraging smoking among certain consumer groups), how certain industrial practices are depleting natural resources, and how decisions to relocate plants leave large numbers of unemployed workers and undercut local economies. Thus rationalist evaluation refuses to acknowledge the impact of the firm's activities on stakeholders and the social community at large.

Finally, the rationalist framework has been criticized on the basis of its treatment of the people who work in industrial organizations. Critics argue that within this framework, the sole worth of the worker lies in his or her being able to meet the knowledge and skill specifications required to perform a specialized task efficiently. Workers are thus fragmented into separate and discrete bundles of skills and cognitive capacities that become inputs to the production process. Managers too are hired for their ability to use specialized skills to guide the organization toward its goals. The managerial technologies presume that it does not matter who utilizes them so long as they are used correctly and skillfully. When conducted "by the book," for example, management-by-objectives is supposed to promote the organization's productivity and efficiency regardless of the individual doing the managing.

The deployment of human beings as inputs has been criticized on both normative and practical grounds. Normatively, critics charge that this treatment objectifies people—thus devaluing their distinctively human characteristics and alienating them from their work life and, ultimately, from one another. Alienation in turn encourages people to avoid personal responsibility for the consequences of their actions. This loss of responsibility diminishes the capacity of individuals to grow and develop their humanness—it results in a society of "soulless" men and women.

Practically speaking, the turbulent and complex economic environment has created problems calling for comprehensive and bold solutions. Consequently, the demarcation between managerial decision and technical solution has become blurred. This blurring has created new human resource needs for organizations. Managers and line staff are now needed who are analytical, interpretive, problem oriented, creative, self-motivated, and responsible, people who have the courage to risk even dramatic change and innovation. Organizations that value such characteristics and restructure to take advantage of them are better able to respond to environmental problems—and, in doing so, to provide opportunities for exercising unique individuality and humanness (Levinson, 1980; Pfeffer, 1981).

These concerns and criticisms certainly warrant the examination of other theoretical contexts from which evaluations might be conducted to serve business and industrial organizations, especially those in transition. Sociotechnical theory offers one such alternative. Indeed, it provides a role for evaluation that has promise for overcoming the inadequacies of the rational framework.

The Sociotechnical Framework

Whereas the rational framework emerged from Anglo-American political theories, sociotechnical theory has its roots in the German expressivist tradition. Like the rational framework, the sociotechnical framework has a distinctive conception of human nature that is ultimately extended to explain organizational dynamics. In the sociotechnical framework, humans are viewed as inherently social beings whose natural habitat is the social community. Indeed, individuality only emerges within and in contradistinction to the relations between the individual and other social members.

Humans are also purposeful in nature and express their intentions through activity, including the activity of creating socially shared meanings, norms, and institutions. In this sense, they are productive beings whose need "to do" is as central to their makeup as are their biological drives and requirements. In their purposive productivity, humans are continuously transforming their social and natural environment. Yet there is a reflexive relation between the two. As individuals create their social reality, this reality assumes an objective status which in turn defines the modes of human expression, knowledge, and action available to the society's members at that point in history.

This conceptualization of the social nature of individuals leads to a dramatically different view of organizations than that afforded by the atomistic, individualistic, and goal-directed rational model. In the rational framework, the corporate organization is itself an instrument to be employed for goal attainment. In the sociotechnical framework, the organization is the embodiment of socially organized relations and serves as a primary context in which humans exercise their individual and social natures. The organization thus serves as a medium that has intrinsic worth above and beyond the goods, services, and profits it generates (Trist, 1982; Davis, 1977).

Like society itself, the organization is structured into components that are functionally interdependent and constitutive of the organization as a whole. Rather than being simply the sum of its parts, the organization is instead an integrated reflection of its internal relations and processes. Rather than being goal-directed like rationalist organizations, the sociotechnical firm is teleological in its purposiveness. It is teleological in the sense that its activities, decisions, and outcomes can only be made intelligible by interpreting them in terms of the purposes they serve. Action and intent are conceptually interrelated. Indeed, action is the expression of intent. Because the organization comprises the social understandings and interrelatedness of the people affected by it, its activity must be viewed in light of the constitutive interests and intentions of these same individuals (Herbst, 1974; Faucheux, Amado, and Laurent, 1982).

The constitutive nature of the organization means that decision making in the sociotechnical framework is much more decentralized and pluralistic than in the rational framework. This does not mean that every stakeholder must be involved in each and every decision. Rather, it means that those whose interests are directly involved in a problem or decision outcome have the opportunity to participate in developing that outcome.

Consequently, the distinction between decision making and implementation is more blurred. Because nonmanagerial personnel are involved in decision-making processes, an emphasis is placed on hiring personnel who have general skills in problem solving, decision making, critique, and analysis as well as technical skills. Since decision making is somewhat decentralized, accountability is decentralized as well. Consequently, personnel are expected to be self-supervisory and self-motivated. Work or task groups often span functional areas to work on solutions. As a consequence, the structural divisions between components are more permeable, more flexible, and more subject to change as the organization adapts to the requirements of problem solving.

In contrast to the rational model's perspective, sociotechnical theory views the firm as a constituent part of the greater economic and social system in which it operates. As a constituent part, the firm contributes to the activity of forming the environment. In turn, the environment takes on an objective existence by presenting the firm with economic, social, legal, and technological constraints and opportunities. Thus there is continuous interaction between organization and environment such that a functional interdependence between the two evolves which blurs or shifts the boundaries separating them. As a result of the assumptions dealing with boundary permeability, diffusion, and exchange, sociotechnical theorists treat organizations as "open systems" that are analogous to biological organisms (Morgan, 1986; Trist, 1982).

As in the rational framework, human knowledge has a distinctive role to play in the sociotechnical framework. A major assumption of the sociotechnical perspective is that human interests and purposes are reflected and expressed in knowledge—including the ways in which it is obtained and transferred and the ways in which it is used or applied. Technical knowledge is aimed at enabling humans to shape nature to conform to their needs and wants. Social knowledge is oriented toward identifying those social expressions (norms, institutions, practices) that are consistent with and support the conditions necessary for the exercise of humanness.

Unlike Hempel's separation of instrumental versus categorical knowledge, social and technical knowledge are conceptually interdependent. Thus while developments in technical knowledge may make it possible for a society to fulfill new human needs, prevailing forms of social interaction may work against the transformations in social organization necessary to actualize the technical innovation. Conversely, social norms and institutions may prevent the creation of new modes of technical thought and expression. Sociotechnical theory represents, as its name suggests, an attempt to advance both types of knowledge in a reflective and constructive manner.

Having provided a brief sketch of the sociotechnical framework, I want to address the role defined for evaluation within this framework. However, I have limited this discussion to those aspects of the evaluator's role that have a direct bearing on criticisms of the rational framework and rationalist evaluation noted earlier.

First, it can be claimed that, generally speaking, the sociotechnical framework provides a set of assumptions that are more in line with the current environment in which corporate organizations must operate. The sociotechnical framework assumes a turbulent and interdependent environment and, consequently, prescribes an organizational structure that allows for the rapid and flexible response to sudden shifts of market, financial, consumer, technological, and economic forces. Moreover, the philosophical orientation underlying the framework encourages new modalities of thought and action. The framework thus frees the evaluator from having to operate along rigid, compartmentalized lines of inquiry and allows him or her to let the context define the analysis rather than vice versa. Indeed, the sociotechnical framework encourages the evaluator to interpret the organization in holistic terms in order to identify and analyze real or potential problems. Moreover, the notions of transition, evolution, and transformation are embedded in the sociotechnical interpretation of organizational life. Therefore, evaluation results that lead to recommendations for restructuring of internal functions and responsibilities are not perceived to be as revolutionary or impractical as would be the case in the rational framework.

Philosophically, the sociotechnical framework demands that evaluation be openly normative as well as practical. After all, the intelligibility of the framework derives from its interpretation of individuals as teleological beings in need of exercising their human capacities (for example, the capacity to reflect critically on the fulfillment of individual needs within the social setting). Moreover, the sociotechnical account of the relation between human knowledge and human interests forces a consideration of the value of social-technical practices and institutions for human actualization. The framework does not so much stipulate the content of that expression as it gives people responsibility for considering this issue in social as well as individualistic terms. Evaluators cannot excuse themselves from this responsibility. In the sociotechnical framework, they must interpret organizational phenomena within the dialectical categories of technical and social interests.

The treatment of the firm as an open system also means that evaluation has a substantive as well as instrumental role to play in the sociotechnical organization. In positing a functionally interdependent relationship between the firm and its environment and in assuming that the firm contributes to defining its environment, sociotechnical theorists actually extend the firm's accountability for its impact on the environment. In this case, impact might encompass the effects of the firm's production processes on the natural environment. It might also encompass the long-term effect of its goods and services on the overall well-being of consumers. Ultimately, it also includes the social understandings, social relations, and social institutions that organizational activities help to sustain or transform.

Unlike its rationalist counterpart, sociotechnical evaluation must be responsive to multiple interests within the organization rather than to management alone. This requirement follows from its basic assumption that the organization is composed of the multiple and diverse interests that carry out organizational activities and by way of which the organization has meaning. All interests are equally important insofar as they are constitutive of the whole. In the sociotechnical framework, moreover, authority and accountability for decision making are pluralistic and cut across traditional management/labor distinctions. Thus the "need to know" cuts across a diversity of interests directly affected by the decision, strategy, or process under evaluation.

The design of the sociotechnical workplace provides management and employees alike with a context that encourages their social relatedness and, in its flexibility, encourages self-defining and self-learning activities. Moreover, its participatory nature encourages them to assume responsibility. The establishment of work groups reinforces the social aspect of work and provides an opportunity for personnel to strengthen their social consciousness. In enhancing social consciousness and social responsibility, the sociotechnical design of work ultimately directs both managers and line staff to consider the social appropriateness and worth of organizational actions.

Summary

I have attempted to serve several purposes in this chapter. First, I have indicated the ways in which theoretical frameworks dictate the role that evaluation can serve. Second, by focusing on two alternative organizational frameworks, I have tried to suggest the functions that evaluation can legitimately serve in assisting business and industry. Third, I have argued that the predominant framework used in organizational research and practice may now be obsolete, or at least inadequate, for purposes of allowing evaluations that are meaningful, fair, and socially responsible. Although the sociotechnical framework may not provide the only or even the best alternative to the rational framework, it does show much promise for overcoming some of the difficulties of evaluation associated with the rational framework.

References

Argyris, C. Reasoning, Learning, and Action. San Francisco: Jossey-Bass, 1982.
Calingo, L.M.R., Perloff, R., and Bryant, F. B. "Thinking Strategically About Private Sector Evaluation: The Key Issues." In R. F. Conner, D. G. Altman, and C. Jackson (eds.), Evaluation Studies Review Annual, Vol. 9. Newbury Park, Calif.: Sage, 1984.

Clark, D. L. "Emerging Paradigms in Organizational Theory and Research." In Y. S. Lincoln (ed.), *Organizational Theory and Inquiry: The Paradigm Revolution.* Newbury Park, Calif.: Sage, 1985.

Davis, L. E. "Enhancing the Quality of Working Life: Developments in the United States." *International Labour Review,* 1977, *116* (1), 53-65.

Downs, A. *An Economic Theory of Democracy.* New York: Harper & Row, 1957.

Dreitzel, H. P. "Social Science and the Problem of Rationality." In I. Katznelson, G. Adams, P. Brenner, and A. Wolfe (eds.), *The Politics and Society Reader.* New York: McKay, 1974.

Faucheux, C., Amado, G., and Laurent, A. "Organizational Development and Change." *Annual Review of Psychology,* 1982, *33,* 343-370.

Hempel, C. G. "Science and Human Values." In C. G. Hempel (ed.), *Aspects of Scientific Explanation and Other Essays in the Philosophy of Science.* New York: Free Press, 1965.

Herbst, P. G. *Socio-Technical Design.* London: Tavistock, 1974.

Levinson, H. "Criteria for Choosing Chief Executives." *Harvard Business Review,* July-August 1980, pp. 113-120.

Lincoln, Y. S. *Organizational Theory and Inquiry: The Paradigm Revolution.* Newbury Park, Calif.: Sage, 1985.

Morgan, G. *Images of Organization.* Newbury Park, Calif.: Sage, 1986.

Patterson, J. L., Purkey, S. C., and Parker, J. V. *Productive School Systems for a Nonrational World.* Alexandria, Va.: Association for Supervision and Curriculum Development, 1986.

Peters, T. J., and Waterman, R. H. *In Search of Excellence.* New York: Harper & Row, 1982.

Pfeffer, J. "Management as Symbolic Action: The Creation and Maintenance of Organizational Paradigms." *Research in Organizational Behavior,* 1981, *3,* 1-52.

Rosen, M. "Organizational Praxis: Topography and Critique." Paper presented at the Conference on Critical Perspectives in Organization Analysis, New York, September 5-7, 1985.

Taylor, C. "Neutrality in Political Science." In W. E. Connolly and G. Gordons (eds.), *Social Structures and Political Theory.* Lexington, Mass.: Heath, 1974.

Trist, E. "The Evolution of Sociotechnical Systems as Conceptual Framework and as an Action Research Program." In A. H. Van de Ven and W. F. Joyce (eds.), *Perspectives on Organization Design and Behavior.* New York: Wiley, 1982.

Weick, K. E. "Educational Organizations as Loosely Coupled Systems." *Administrative Science Quarterly,* 1976, *21,* 1-19.

Weiss, C. H. "The Stakeholder Approach to Evaluation: Origins and Promise." In A. S. Bryk (ed.), *Stakeholder-Based Evaluation.* New Directions for Program Evaluation, no. 17. San Francisco: Jossey-Bass, 1983.

Joanne Farley heads her own consulting practice, Farley & Associates, which specializes in organizational development and evaluation.

Moral inquiry cannot become a practical force in either evaluation or business unless we rethink our current notion of evaluation as scientifically conceived social inquiry and our idea that business is an instrumentality.

Evaluation as Moral Critique

Thomas A. Schwandt

It is a truism that, with few exceptions, the character and temperament (or ethos, if you will) of evaluation in business and industry are drawn from the social sciences. Evaluation models as well as conceptions of the evaluator's role and day-to-day evaluation practice issue from images of the technically competent, politically savvy, expert social scientist who serves the information and decision-making needs of business managers. This understanding of evaluation offers a comfortable fit with the classic view of business organizations as economic, amoral institutions principally concerned with adjusting means to ends in order to maximize profits. Evaluation is a tool for examining the utility, efficacy, and cost effectiveness of various means. This union of scientific and instrumental conceptions of evaluation with the technocratic rationality of business organizations helps explain the authoritativeness of both the evaluation expert and his or her counterpart, the business manager.

In this chapter, I invite readers to consider an alternative conceptualization of evaluation and an alternative scenario about the relationship between business and evaluation. The first section sketches the dominant notion that evaluation is a technical undertaking and presents the complementary view of business as an amoral instrumentality. It demonstrates why moral analysis is not a practical force in evaluation and management. The discussion then shifts to considering both evaluation and business in a new key. Here I outline some developments that might make it possible to view organizations as moral agents capable of organizing for moral as well as economic purposes. In addition, this section offers some thoughts on the possibility of viewing evaluation as a form of moral critique arising from the traditions of social thought rather than social science.

NEW DIRECTIONS FOR PROGRAM EVALUATION, no. 49, Spring 1991 © Jossey-Bass Inc., Publishers

Current Perspectives

Evaluation as a Technical Practice. Wrangling over qualitative versus quantitative approaches to evaluation has of late given way to discussions about the service versus academic orientation of evaluators (Cordray and Lipsey, 1987; Schwandt, 1990)—what Patton (1988b) has labeled the practice/action paradigm versus the research/truth paradigm. At first blush it appears that this difference provides us with a meaningful way of distinguishing two different kinds of practice. Although this notion may be useful in pointing out that evaluators with different organizational allegiances (business versus academia, for example), frame their evaluation practice in keeping with the demands of different institutional and professional requirements, the distinction is fundamentally artificial.

This is so because both views—from Patton's (1986) service-oriented approach to Rossi and Freeman's (1982) social science evaluation research model—share a utilitarian view of evaluation. Although acknowledging that evaluation unfolds in a political milieu, both orientations are predominantly technocratic. That is, they largely ignore moral dimensions in evaluating policies and programs—assuming instead that the key to sound practice is to be found in clarifying types of decisions to be made, matching methods to problems, making accurate analyses, improving the usefulness of findings, and so forth. Both promote a professional image of the evaluator as an expert technical adviser and defend the power of analytic reason to transform human affairs.

Examining how current concepts of evaluation have developed this particular orientation is beyond the scope of this chapter. The development of evaluation and policy analysis within the tradition of political, economic, social, and philosophical thought known as liberalism—characterized by its instrumental view of social relationships, its utilitarian theory of value, and its endorsement of an empirical-analytic science of human affairs—has been discussed extensively elsewhere. (See, for example, the essays by Schwandt, 1989, and Sullivan, 1983, as well as the more detailed analyses of MacIntyre, 1984; Rein, 1976; Sandel, 1982; Sullivan, 1986; and Tribe, 1976.)

The exclusion of moral dimensions from evaluation persists in part because of the mistaken but pervasive belief that moral judgments are inherently subjective expressions of personal preference and, therefore, incapable of rational justification. Yet Ericson's (1990) recent account of the systematic treatment of social justice is only one example demonstrating how moral analysis is anything but irrational. Amy's (1984) study of the relationship between policy analysis and ethics can be readily adapted to provide us with additional insight into why the moral dimensions of evaluation practice are neglected. He claims that moral inquiry is avoided because it threatens the professional and political interests of administrators and policy analysts in at least four ways.

First, it is a threat to the evaluator/client relationship. Because moral analysis inevitably raises questions about current policy, it threatens the smooth pursuit of the dominant values of the organization. Clients are not likely to look favorably on evaluators who raise questions about goals and values that are accepted by the client and the organization itself. The evaluator is expected to work within the consensus of ongoing programs and policies.

Second, if evaluators were to engage in moral analysis, they would likely undermine their professional image as technical experts. The participation of evaluators in examining programs and policies is politically legitimate precisely because they are skilled at drawing the line between questions of fact and value. Their involvement is built on a view of knowledge as *techne* (craft knowledge)—that is, knowledge *about* programs or policies that is ahistorical and requires neither participation nor involvement. To admit that programs and policies should be investigated using moral assumptions, and not simply scientific assumptions, threatens the very foundations of evaluation as a professional service.

Third, Amy claims that the style of moral analysis conflicts with the desire of administrators and managers to maintain a technocratic image. They prefer to be perceived as making rational decisions based on hard data. Since they often (mistakenly) believe that values are nothing but subjective preferences, it would weaken their image to be seen debating forms of moral reasoning. Moral analysis undermines the illusion of non-political, scientifically managed decision making.

Finally, managers and evaluators may be reluctant to engage in moral analysis because they are not interested in questioning the basic tenets of liberal capitalist ideology that form the backdrop for the development of policies and programs in business, industry, and government. As Amy (p. 585) points out, instead of seeing politics—whether in private corporations or in public agencies—as involving the debate over the basic characteristics of our political, economic, and social system, we "have always preferred to portray politics more as a matter of practical problem-solving. . . . The assumption is that current economic and political arrangements are basically justified."

Therefore, it is not surprising that in recent writing on evaluation in business and industry (Brinkerhoff, 1989a; May, Moore, and Zammit, 1987) there is virtually no mention of the role of evaluation in investigating normative concerns. Rather, writers begin with the assumption that the framework for business decision making embraces the economic values of efficiency and effectiveness in attaining business goals (Swanson, 1989). Since business goals, issues, or problems are taken as a given, evaluation should serve a quality assurance or quality control function in helping managers address those goals or problems (Brandenburg, 1989). In discussing training evaluation, Brinkerhoff (1989b, p. 19) makes the point succinctly: "The role of evaluation is to ensure that training resources are effectively deployed to best serve strategic needs, and that training operations deliver optimum value [that is, return on investment]." In discussing how best to position an internal evaluation unit within a business and convince management of its value, Nowakowski (1989, p. 55) advises that one should "put evaluation to work to maximize return on committed resources. At any point in time, most organizational resources are committed to specified goals. Having made these commitments, organizational attention is focused rightly on meeting those goals to obtain expected returns. Internal evaluation resources should be similarly focused. The majority of evaluation resources should be allocated to obtaining and providing data to help maximize goal attainment."

These commentators on the role of evaluation in business and industry take the stance that evaluation can be considered valuable only if it is linked to the business ethos. This view, however, is not limited to business and industry. If we are to believe a formidable advocate for the field as a whole, evaluation should in fact be better assimilated to the modes of interaction (that is, marketing and selling) and patterns of thought (that is, accountability, "closing the sale") characteristic of the marketplace and the bureaucracies (Patton, 1988a).

Business as an Amoral Instrumentality. The idea that evaluation is a technical enterprise dovetails nicely with beliefs about corporations as instrumentalities and the view that business managers are strategic and analytical administrators with no particular responsibility for stewardship over noneconomic values. We see these beliefs expressed in the collection of papers on business evaluation noted earlier: "The mission and goal of business and industry are to maximize the economic return on investment through the production and sale of goods and services" (Swanson, 1989, p. 71); "the task of management is to manage resources in response to external pressures and opportunities and to internal goals, needs, and capabilities" (Brethower, 1989, p. 32).

Before considering this view of organizations directly, it is important to note that it is grounded in a conception of individuals and society that stretches from Machiavelli through Hobbes and Locke. As Klein (1988, p. 66) explains, one of the central tenets of modern political philosophy is that human beings are incapable of organizing a community based on virtue (human excellence in the classical view) and that the most we can expect from the great majority of people is narrow self-interest. Our innate selfish drives, the most fundamental of which is self-preservation, form the basis for civil society. In Klein's words: "Materialism (comfortable self-preservation), not justice or virtue, is our goal, and power is the means of securing it" (p. 67).

In this Machiavellian view of society, where people are driven by narrow self-interest, Klein (p. 67) explains that the classical virtues cannot exist within an organization "except as mere shams of virtue: For example, temperance becomes the obedience, loyalty, docility, and concern for security of what William Whyte called the organization man. Courage degenerates into excessive cutthroat competitiveness. . . . Wisdom . . . becomes the narrow cleverness of the person who can find the so-called practical solutions to immediate, concrete problems. . . . Justice becomes . . . a necessary evil; it is determined by what is lawful and enforced by power."

Consistent with this tradition of thought is the view that corporations are collectives formally organized for economic purposes. Klein (p. 62) refers to the work of John Ladd, who argues that corporations should be treated not as members of the moral community but as amoral instrumentalities dedicated to the goals of producing goods and services efficiently, maximizing profit, and conducting business in a lawful manner. According to Ladd, corporate actions are subject only to the standard of "rational efficiency (utility)" in evaluating whether the corporation has employed the correct means to achieve its objectives. Corporate rationality is defined strictly in terms of determining means not ends.

Klein (p. 62) explains that the moral views of society will indeed be considered in making corporate judgments—but "only because [and only to the extent that] they are pertinent to determining means to goals." Moral evaluations of the organization's goals and actions may be made from outside the corporation, but they are essentially irrelevant to the organization itself. Corporations are concerned with morality only to the extent that they are acting lawfully; in other words, legal and moral obligations are regarded as equivalent. Corporations can only be brought into line with the demands of morality through the use of sanctions. Because the organization is a machine, Ladd (cited in Klein, 1988, p. 63) argues that "the only way to make the rights and interests of individuals . . . logically relevant to organizational decision-making is to convert them into pressures of one sort or another, e.g., to bring the pressure of law or public opinion to bear on the organization. Such pressures would then be introduced into the rational decision-making as limiting operating conditions."

Ladd admits, and Klein concurs, that a kind of alienation arises from the fact that members of corporations live according to a double standard— amorally as members of the organization and morally as private persons. Klein (p. 63) describes the consequences of this alienation as follows: "The more we immerse ourselves in social actions, the more we tend to use amoral [that is, strictly rational], rather than moral, social standards as the basis for decisions and evaluations of actions. The administrator's point of view breeds alienation (from people and moral decisions); the moral point of view is essentially people oriented."

An Alternative Perspective

The foregoing scenario presents a rather formidable barrier to the possibility of introducing moral analysis as a practical force in either evaluation practice or business decision making. Yet there are signs that "moral business" and "moral evaluation" may not be oxymora. An optimistic view would suggest that we are in a state of transition in our thinking about both evaluation and business with respect to the role of moral inquiry.

On the Possibility of Moral Inquiry in Business. Although the issues are far from settled, three developments highlight new understandings about corporations and social responsibility. The first centers on shifting perceptions of the goal of business. Peter Drucker (1980) has been a major voice in arguing that although many people both inside and outside corporations believe that the goal of business is to maximize profit, this is a delusion. Profit, Drucker claims, is the cost of staying in business. Supplying better and more economic goods and services is the proper goal of business; profit is the cost of risk, change, and innovation required to achieve that goal.

Drucker has also been influential in arguing that business enterprises can no longer be viewed as single-purpose institutions whose activity is justified solely in terms of one specific area of contribution and performance—namely, economic. He argues that all institutions, including corporations, "have progressively become carriers of social purpose, social values, social effectiveness. Therefore they have become politicized. They cannot justify themselves any longer in terms of their own contribution areas alone; all of them have to justify themselves now in terms of the impacts they have on society overall" (p. 207).

Drucker's views are controversial. His position contrasts sharply with that of Milton Friedman, for example, who has denounced the concern for social responsibility as fundamentally subversive. "There is one and only one social responsibility of business," writes Friedman (1962, p. 133), "to use its resources and engage in activities designed to increase its profits so long as it . . . engages in open and free competition without deception or fraud." Yet there has been progress in exploring the notion of corporate social responsibility (see, for example, Andrews, 1975). To the extent that these views gain a foothold in management education and training programs, they may be instrumental in helping corporations rethink their views of what it means to do business. This is far from a critique of liberal capitalist society or a call for the subordination of the economic realm to the political, of course, but it could be an avenue for reconsidering the moral context of economic life.

A second development that supports the possibility of opening a dialogue about moral inquiry in business is the recent shift in management theory. The traditional conception of business voiced by Milton Friedman contrasts with modern theories of management. (See, for example, Ouchi, 1981; Peters and Waterman, 1982.) According to Klein (1988, p. 61), these new theories contend that "managers should balance the legitimate, though often competing, claims of shareholders, customers, employees, suppliers, and the general public in a just or fair manner." Further, "business should emphasize quality goods and services rather than short-term profits, provide opportunities for employees to dedicate themselves to values that are noble . . . and develop management that has a concern for people." Klein claims that these views are "morally sounder" than the traditional view because of their other-regarding character.

A third development signifying an interest in the role of moral inquiry in business is the debate unfolding in the field of business ethics (Curtler, 1986; Donaldson and Werhane, 1988) over whether we can properly view corporations as moral agents (Klein, 1988; Skidd, 1988). While the arguments are too involved to relate in this brief chapter, they center on whether it is possible to develop an analogy between corporations and persons and thereby defend the view that "organizational agents such as corporations should be no more or less morally responsible (rational, self-interested, altruistic) than ordinary persons" (Goodpaster and Matthews cited in Klein, 1988, p. 58) or that corporations should be treated as "members in full standing of the moral community" (French cited in Klein, 1988, p. 55).

The issue is far from settled, and there are those (such as Ladd) who think it unlikely that a persuasive alternative to a Machiavellian or Hobbesian view is possible. For them, the notion of a moral organization is an oxymoron; the classical virtues function in organizations only in the degenerate form described earlier by Klein. Hence, they argue, there is little hope of introducing notions of moral responsibility in corporate actions.

On the Possibility of Evaluation as Moral Critique. Defenders of the technical view of evaluation will argue that moral inquiry and evaluation are two distinct spheres of human activity—the former philosophical, the latter technical. Hence the integrity of each should be preserved because they involve a different craft, require different skills, and serve different roles. (In fact, this very argument has been made to counter the notion of the applied humanities and to justify the separation of the humanities and the social sciences; see Hastings Center, 1984.)

Yet it seems undeniable that evaluation, policy analysis, and policymaking are not simply technical undertakings. As recent work by Guba and Lincoln (1989), House (1988). Simons (1987), Stake (1986), Sirotnik (1990), and others demonstrates, social vision, values, and awareness of tradition are part of its consciousness as a social practice. Further, evaluation cannot be immune to the controversy surrounding the blurring of boundaries in the disciplines that have shaped its character, to arguments that call for viewing social science inquiry as continuous with inquiry in the humanities, and to concerns for renewing a sense of social science as public philosophy.

If we cling to the view that evaluation is but an extension of traditional notions of social science, then imagining a role for the evaluator as moral critic will be ill-advised at best and at worst heretical. But if we begin to view evaluation as one of the ways we seek to interpret ourselves to ourselves, this conception becomes less improbable. To reorient evaluation in this way will require several considerations. First, we must explore the implications of the recovery of the Aristotelian notion of *praxis* (versus *techne*) for the kind of knowledge about human affairs that we seek in doing evaluation. A focus on craft knowledge must at least be supplemented with an understanding of how and why we conduct evaluation for the purpose of gaining insight into how to live.

Second, we must examine the professional image of evaluators as experts and the very notion of expert itself. There is great danger, of course, in replacing the image of the evaluator as expert social scientist with the image of evaluator as expert moralist. How can evaluators provide different modes of understanding and analysis, guidance, criticism, and advice to clients without clothing it all in the image of expert?

Third, we might attend to a lesson taught by feminist writers who make the so-called variable of gender into a theoretical category that in turn shapes the nature and purpose of investigations. The analogue for evaluators is discussing how we can make ethics and morality theoretical categories, and not simply variables, in our evaluation practice.

Fourth, we must explore the use of moral vocabularies (Stout, 1988) other than the vocabulary of rights, of cost-benefit analysis, of legal responsibility. We must reconsider the vocabulary of the virtues (wisdom, justice, temperance, courage) and examine how both the social practice of evaluation itself and the practices it investigates are ordered toward attaining them.

Fifth, we must deepen our understanding of what it means to cultivate an "evaluative cast of mind" among managers and policymakers (Weiss, 1988, p. 27). That disposition must be expanded to include not only skepticism of received wisdom and a willingness to examine program assumptions but also an interest in understanding that evaluation aims at achieving insight and awareness into what it means to live a human life. This, in turn, involves a deepening of the role of evaluator as educator. Whether as "public scientist" (Cronbach and others, 1980) or fourth-generation evaluator (Guba and Lincoln, 1989), the evaluator must be capable of facilitating an exploration of moral issues.

Moral inquiry is unlikely to become an integral part of evaluation in business and industry unless evaluators and business managers are able to alter their thinking about evaluation as scientifically conceived social inquiry while simultaneously adjusting their views of the nature of business.

References

Amy, D. J. "Why Policy Analysis and Ethics Are Incompatible." *Journal of Policy Analysis and Management,* 1984, 3 (4), 573–591.

Andrews, K. R. "Can the Best Corporations Be Made 'Moral'?" In *Harvard Business Review: On Management.* New York: Harper & Row, 1975.

Brandenburg, D. C. "Evaluation and Business Issues: Tools for Management Decision Making." In R. O. Brinkerhoff (ed.), *Evaluating Training Programs in Business and Industry.* New Directions for Program Evaluation, no. 44. San Francisco: Jossey-Bass, 1989.

Brethower, D. M. "Evaluating the Merit and Worth of Sales Training: Asking the Right Questions." In R. O. Brinkerhoff (ed.), *Evaluating Training Programs in Business and Industry.* New Directions for Program Evaluation, no. 44. San Francisco: Jossey-Bass, 1989.

Brinkerhoff, R. O. (ed.). *Evaluating Training Programs in Business and Industry.* New Directions for Program Evaluation, no. 44. San Francisco: Jossey-Bass, 1989a.

Brinkerhoff, R. O. "Using Evaluation to Transform Training." In R. O. Brinkerhoff (ed.), *Evaluating Training Programs in Business and Industry.* New Directions for Program Evaluation, no. 44. San Francisco: Jossey-Bass, 1989b.

Cordray, D. S., and Lipsey, M. W. "Evaluation Studies for 1986: Program Evaluation and Program Research." In D. S. Cordray and M. W. Lipsey (eds.), *Evaluation Studies Review Annual,* Vol. 11. Newbury Park, Calif.: Sage, 1987.

Cronbach, L. J., and others. *Toward Reform of Program Evaluation: Aims, Methods, and Institutional Arrangements.* San Francisco: Jossey-Bass, 1980.

Curtler, H. (ed.). *Shame, Responsibility and the Corporation.* New York: Haven, 1986.

Donaldson, T., and Werhane, P. H. (eds.). *Ethical Issues in Business: A Philosophical Approach.* Englewood Cliffs, N.J.: Prentice-Hall, 1988.

Drucker, P. F. *Managing in Turbulent Times.* New York: Harper & Row, 1980.

Ericson, D. P. "Social Justice, Evaluation, and the Educational System." In K. A. Sirotnik (ed.), *Evaluation and Social Justice: Issues in Public Education.* New Directions for Program Evaluation, no. 45. San Francisco: Jossey-Bass, 1990.

Friedman, M. *Capitalism and Freedom.* Chicago: University of Chicago Press, 1962.

Guba, E. G., and Lincoln, Y. S. *Fourth Generation Evaluation.* Newbury Park, Calif.: Sage, 1989.

Hastings Center. *On the Uses of the Humanities: Vision and Application.* Hastings-on-Hudson, N.Y.: Hastings Center, 1984.

House, E. R. *Jesse Jackson and the Politics of Charisma: The Rise and Fall of the PUSH/Excel Program.* Boulder, Colo.: Westview Press, 1988.

Klein, S. "Is a Moral Organization Possible?" *Business and Professional Ethics Journal,* 1988, 7 (1), 51–73.

MacIntyre, A. *After Virtue.* (2nd ed.) Notre Dame, Ind.: University of Notre Dame, 1984.

May, L. S., Moore, C. A., and Zammit, S. J. *Evaluating Business and Industry Training.* Boston: Kluwer-Nijhoff, 1987.

Nowakowski, A. C. "Strategy for Internal Evaluators." In R. O. Brinkerhoff (ed.), *Evaluating Training Programs in Business and Industry.* New Directions for Program Evaluation, no. 44. San Francisco: Jossey-Bass, 1989.

Ouchi, W. G. *Theory Z.* Reading, Mass.: Addison-Wesley, 1981.

Patton, M. Q. *Utilization-Focused Evaluation.* (2nd ed.) Newbury Park, Calif.: Sage, 1986.

Patton, M. Q. "The Evaluator's Responsibility for Utilization." *Evaluation Practice,* 1988a, 9 (2), 5–24.

Patton, M. Q. "Politics and Evaluation." *Evaluation Practice,* 1988b, 9 (1), 89–94.

Peters, T. H., and Waterman, R. H., Jr. *In Search of Excellence.* New York: Harper & Row, 1982.

Rein, M. *Social Science and Public Policy.* New York: Penguin Books, 1976.

Rossi, P. H., and Freeman, H. E. Evaluation: A Systematic Approach. (2nd ed.) Newbury Park, Calif.: Sage, 1982.

Sandel, M. Liberalism and the Limits of Justice. Cambridge, England: Cambridge University Press, 1982.

Schwandt, T. A. "Recapturing Moral Discourse in Evaluation." Educational Researcher, 1989, 18 (8), 11-16.

Schwandt, T. A. "Defining 'Quality' in Evaluation." Evaluation and Program Planning, 1990, 13 (2), 177-188.

Simons, H. Getting to Know Schools in a Democracy: The Politics and Process of Evaluation. London: Falmer Press, 1987.

Sirotnik, K. A. (ed.). Evaluation and Social Justice: Issues in Public Education. New Directions for Program Evaluation, no. 45. San Francisco: Jossey-Bass, 1990.

Skidd, D.R.A. "Corporate Responsibility: Morality Without Consciousness." Business and Professional Ethics Journal, 1988, 7 (1), 51-73.

Stake, R. E. Quieting Reform. Urbana: University of Illinois Press, 1986.

Stout, J. Ethics After Babel. Boston: Beacon Press, 1988.

Sullivan, W. S. "Beyond Policy Science: The Social Sciences as Moral Sciences." In N. Haan, R. N. Bellah, P. Rabinow, and W. S. Sullivan (eds.), Social Science as Moral Inquiry. New York: Columbia University Press, 1983.

Sullivan, W. S. Reconstructing Public Philosophy. Berkeley, Calif.: University of California Press, 1986.

Swanson, R. A. "Everything Important in Business and Industry Is Evaluated." In R. O. Brinkerhoff (ed.), Evaluating Training Programs in Business and Industry. New Directions for Program Evaluation, no. 44. San Francisco: Jossey-Bass, 1989.

Tribe, L. (ed.). When Values Conflict. Cambridge, Mass.: Ballinger, 1976.

Weiss, C. H. "If Program Decisions Hinged Only on Information: A Response to Patton." Evaluation Practice, 1988, 9 (3), 15-28.

Thomas A. Schwandt is associate professor in the Educational Inquiry Methodology Program, School of Education, Indiana University, Bloomington.

Immersed in the traditional ideology of business management, consultants to organizations are unlikely to affect the transformation of management philosophy and practice without deconstructing, interpreting, and reframing the organization's ideology.

Transforming Management Philosophy: Beyond the Illusion of Change

Colleen L. Larson

The recent literature in management, organization development, and evaluation is replete with examples of dynamic leaders transforming management and decision-making practices in business and industry. (See Peters, 1987; Peters and Waterman, 1982; Moss Kanter, 1983.) Much of this literature lauds the growing trend in corporations toward implementing participative decision-making practices, increasing democratization on the shop floor, and adopting more collaborative problem-solving processes in the workplace.

Although these efforts to transform management philosophy and practice are encouraging, organization consultants who are retained to assess and make recommendations for furthering these initiatives must do so critically. Academics have expressed concern about human needs and interests in organizations for over fifty years (Mayo, 1933; Follett, 1941; McGregor, 1960). However, democratic practices have never been central to decision making in business and industry; therefore, transformation to a participative philosophy requires significant change in traditional business management practices.

This chapter examines the emerging trend of adopting participative management practices in many business organizations, noting both the structural and the ideological factors that impede the acceptance of participative management in traditional organizations. As we shall see, much of what has been accomplished in the name of participative management, representative democracy, and bottom-up reform in business corporations remains grounded in traditional management ideology—and this ideology is contrary to the participative management philosophy. After examining the traditional nature of evaluative inquiry for interpreting and transforming management philosophy and practice, I suggest a new role for evaluators of such initiatives.

Throughout the chapter I use the term *ideology* to mean the traditional operating systems, symbols, beliefs, values, and assumptions that undergird management behavior and practice. Since many of these traditional values are contradictory to the values that must undergird a participative management philosophy, they must be transformed if organizations are to reap the benefits of more inclusive management systems. I also use the terms *participative management, participative practices,* and *authentic participation.* Behind each of these terms is the assumption that workers are integrally engaged in democratic decision making that affects the core management philosophy and practice of the organization. Such practices require that all human beings be viewed as moral agents with central roles in determining the future direction of the organizations in which they work (Sirotnik and Oakes, 1990; McCarthy, 1978).

Four major assertions are advanced here. First, transformation of management philosophy and practice must be made at the core of organizational behavior and beliefs. Additive "programs" such as quality circles and employee involvement marginalize the emergent ideology of democratic, participative decision making and reinforce the dominant management ideology. Second, participative management initiatives are often posited as programs to be assessed rather than *systems of thought* undergirded by well-ingrained beliefs, attitudes, interests, and concerns that must be deconstructed, interpreted, and critiqued. This narrow focus for evaluating management transformation initiatives has resulted in findings that focus on method and technique rather than on needed change in traditional management ideology. Third, organization consultants and business leaders functioning within the dominant ideology of traditional management are not likely to see the ideological barriers that impede the infusion of participative and democratic practices in the workplace and are therefore likely to reinforce traditional management beliefs and practices. Fourth, a legitimate role for organization consultants is that of educator and facilitator for deconstructing and interpreting the ideology that undergirds management transformation initiatives. If organizations are to truly transform management philosophy and practice people must critically explore the values, beliefs, fears, and interests that keep them grounded in traditional behavior. Evaluators must engage people in public and critical dialogue about the values, beliefs, attitudes, and interests that undergird their perceptions of *authentic* participation in organizations.

Examining Current Practices

Current evaluation of employee involvement initiatives often fails to recognize the dominant ideology of management as a powerful force that impedes the inculcation of authentic participative practices in organizations. Many writers fail to challenge the existing dominant management ideology or recognize the incompatibility of authentic participation within these organizations. (See Moss Kanter, 1983; Barra, 1983; Schoenberger, 1982; Peters and Waterman, 1982; Thompson, 1980.) As a result, many participative practices have been implemented in organizations but very few have resulted in authentic participation for American workers. Robert Howard criticizes this situation in his book *Brave New Workplace* (1985), where he argues that quality circles are designed to disguise and suppress the problems of people and their need for meaningful work and genuine participation in the workplace. I suggest that current approaches to transforming management decision-making practices are just as likely rooted in the unconscious assumptions of traditional management as they are in any conscious desire to disguise and suppress authentic participation. Equally, evaluators have done little to expose these unconscious values, beliefs, behavior, and practices.

Utilitarian evaluations of participative practices like quality circles predictably result in findings comfortably nestled within the dominant ideology of traditional management. These client-focused (often management-focused) evaluations concentrate on the features of participative practices that exist in organizations (the number and nature of participative circles, the opportunity for clerical and line workers to participate in group settings, the nature of communication within groups, the impact of training on group decision making, the program's strengths and weaknesses). Such instrumental evaluation diverts attention from the ideology that undergirds participative practices and, therefore, fails to analyze the impact of these practices on authentic participation. Further, goal-based assessments of changing management practices often assume that these initiatives are merely "programs" to be assessed and therefore fail to recognize the structural and ideological barriers that preclude their acceptance in the organization at large.

Reflecting Strategy Through Structure

Alfred Chandler (1962) cautioned business leaders that structure follows strategy. His message was to get the strategy straight before designing the structure. Structure does reflect strategy and is, therefore, instructive when examining the inculcation of participative practices in organizations. It is clear that the most pervasive structure used for incorporating participative strategies such as quality circles and quality of worklife practices in business and industry is the parallel organization (Lawler and Mohrman, 1987). The parallel, or collateral, organization is simply a new structure that is added to the formal hierarchical structure—"a supplemental organization coexisting with the usual formal organization" (Zand, 1989, p. 357). The perceived advantages of the parallel organization are that it allows management to experiment with new product lines, business ventures, structures, and groupings without harming the ongoing needs of the business. In the parallel organization, groups of people come together to address opportunities or problems not dealt with in the traditional organization hierarchy.

At the root of the parallel organization is the belief that hierarchy is essential to managing and controlling an organization and its people. Thus the formal organization and all top-down reporting relationships and control mechanisms remain intact. These values are reflective of traditional management ideology. Elliott Jacques (1990, p. 129) echoes the view of many business leaders when he says that "hierarchy is and will remain the only way to structure unified work." This thinking has relegated participative management efforts to the side of business organizations as separate programs, rather than as viable alternatives to conventional management practices within the formal organization.

In theory, the formal (traditional) organization in the collateral structure is supposed to be limited to dealing with problems that are routine, simple, and will not negatively affect people. Therefore, these issues move quickly and efficiently through the formal hierarchy. Problems that are complex, ill-defined, or concern people's rights, roles, or responsibilities require more careful scrutiny and broader input and should therefore be allocated to the parallel (participative) organization. The theory, however, encounters great obstacles in practice. Raymond Boudon (1990) reminds us that we must be careful to differentiate between ideas and the political use to which they are put.

According to Jacques (1990), hierarchy has been the predominant organizational structure for over three thousand years. Hierarchy, power, control, and decision making have become indistinguishably intertwined in the minds of many managers (and employees as well). Managers in organizations have operated within the formal organization hierarchy for all decision making since the birth of industrial life. To many business leaders, effective management means control over people and management control means power within organizations. These operating values are vastly different from those needed in a participative organization.

In a thoughtful book called *Images of Organizations*, Gareth Morgan (1986) describes different lenses for viewing organizations. Two of the lenses he discusses are "organizations as machines" and "organizations as organisms." Organizations viewed as machines are described as closed systems with hierarchical structures grounded in functional or instrumental rationality. This definition describes the traditional organization within a collateral organization structure. He contends that the "mechanistic organization discourages initiative, encouraging people to obey orders and keep their place rather than take an interest, question, and challenge what they are doing. People in a bureaucracy who question the wisdom of conventional practice are viewed more often than not as troublemakers. Therefore, apathy often reigns, as people learn to feel powerless about problems which collectively they understand and ultimately have the power to solve" (p. 37). By way of contrast, the organization as organism metaphor, which more accurately reflects the values of the participative organization, stresses the importance of achieving a balance between strategy, structure, technology, people's commitments and needs, and the external environment. This metaphor, grounded in sociotechnical systems theory and contingency management, focuses on meeting both the technical and social needs of people in organizations.

The notion of a collateral organization assumes that these two structures can coexist. Certainly Rosabeth Moss Kanter (1983, p. 204) suggests that they can: "It is possible for a 'mechanistic' production hierarchy and an 'organic' participative organization to exist side by side, carrying out different but complementary kinds of tasks. These two organization types are not necessarily opposites, but different mechanisms for involving people in organizational tasks." Yet the differences between these two structures, however, are far deeper than "different mechanisms for involving people in organizational tasks." These structures are grounded in conflicting management philosophies and are undergirded by very different assumptions about people and their rights and roles in organizations and decision making.

Management behavior is not a function of being engaged in the formal or the participative side of the collateral organization—it is a function of the ideology that informs the actions of the manager. A transformation in management ideology challenges more than one hundred years of American business tradition. Autocratic leaders will change when the dominant ideology undergirding their behavior is changed. I recall a director of a Fortune 500 manufacturing company who influenced my thinking on this issue. I remember watching this fifty-something executive push hard to have a participative management group accept his solution to a serious problem. He was clearly not used to having to influence people he clearly viewed as subordinates. When the group seemed reluctant to accept his ideas, he ceremoniously removed an imaginary hat from his head and said, "Well, now I have to take off my participative hat and put on my management hat." The message was clear. As a corporate manager, he felt compelled to take control (a value of the dominant ideology) in order to avoid potential errors in "participative" decision making.

Given the conflicting values of the parallel organization and the formal organization, this incident is hardly surprising. Management actions are based on well-ingrained beliefs, values, and expectations. People do not take off and put on new values like they change hats. They cannot simply declare themselves participative managers and then behave that way because they are now on "the participative" side of the organization. For many managers, the traditional organization is the comfortable organization. Though they may venture into participative practices occasionally, when their authority or personal esteem is threatened a quick retreat to the familiarity of the old hierarchy is welcome relief. The coexisting formal organization seemingly serves to protect management from the perceived dangers of authentic participative practices.

Additive change efforts—adding a structure to the untouched traditional structure—seldom bring about a transformation of ideas and practices within the formal organization and at the same time marginalize the importance of participative practices in organization decision making. An employee I interviewed in one organization observed: "There is employee involvement—and then there is the *real* organization. Employees know that the *real* organization is the one in which they are promoted or demoted and reflects the *real* values and beliefs of management in the organization."

The participative organization quickly becomes a second-class program dependent upon top management support within the traditional hierarchy for *meaningful* inclusion in decision making. It is not unusual for important decisions to be safely placed in the hierarchical control of task forces within the formal organization. Problem-solving teams in the participative organization are often limited to such topics as housekeeping, entertainment, and social events, or they are allowed to make low-risk decisions that hold little fascination for managers in the traditional organization. Even when key topics are allocated to the participative structure, these problem-solving teams typically have the authority only to *recommend* solutions. Final decision-making authority remains in the traditional organization and within the control of management. This structure keeps meaningful decision making out of the hands of those at the bottom of the organization while creating the illusion that participative practices are an important and visible part of management philosophy and practice.

Some organizations have taken the risk of infusing participative practices within the formal organization. These initiatives take the form of autonomous work teams and cross-organizational task forces and operate at the core of the formal organization. The work these teams do is crucial to the success of the business. This approach to participative management brings a team of people together to accomplish key tasks and plan new initiatives. Most important, the responsibility for planning, managing, and controlling work is placed directly in the hands of workers—not in the hierarchy of the traditional organization.

Few organizations using participative management through a parallel structure ever evolve to authentic participative initiatives, such as autonomous work teams within the formal organization (Lawler and Mohrman, 1987; Baloff and Doherty, 1989). This finding is not surprising. The parallel structure holds to the myths that people need time to learn participative skills and that participation on quality circle teams and training in group dynamics, communication, and participative management will ultimately reduce managers' reliance upon top-down decision making and lead eventually to authentic participation and meaningful work within the traditional organization. This is a delusion.

This delusion keeps organization consultants and internal change agents gainfully employed "fixing" symptoms rather than identifying the primary obstacle to the implementation of participative practices in organizations. This obstacle is our failure to recognize management transformation initiatives as changes in ideology and philosophy, rather than changes in method and technique.

Cracking the *Illusion* of Change

Evaluation practices that fail to explore the ideological grounding for participative management initiatives reduce the effort to little more than examining the new tools in the technical manager's toolbox. Traditional evaluation practices focus on participative management as a program to be assessed rather than a *system of thought* to be deconstructed, discussed, and interpreted. Viewing management as a socially constructed system of thought is critical to recognizing the values that marginalize participative management practices and perpetuate the traditional management ideology of organizations.

It is important to recognize that we are all immersed in the socially constructed values and beliefs of our society. Therefore, business leaders, organization consultants, and members of the work force are equally likely to function within the dominant ideology of traditionally accepted management philosophy and practice. When organization consultants accept the traditional ideology of management, they may unintentionally reinforce traditional thinking. In the traditional ideology, executives are not expected to share decision-making power. When they do, they are viewed as doing the unexpected. Since consultants often view CEOs and executive managers who implement participative management initiatives as generously extending their privileges to others, they are often reluctant to criticize participative practices that only exist out of the "goodness of an executive's heart." Let me use a common experience to illustrate this point.

Though we are now in the 1990s, nearly thirty years after the liberating turmoil of the 1960s, a young husband gallantly rising to his feet and sweeping up his crying baby to change its diapers is sure to evoke the admiration and praise of relatives and friends. The young man impresses those around him by simply doing what is unexpected in our traditionally patriarchal society. How well or how often he performs this task is seldom addressed. What matters is that he does what others perceive as "above and beyond the call of duty"—or, rather, something that is not perceived as his responsibility in our society. The reactions of relatives and friends clearly reflect dominant societal beliefs about parental roles and responsibilities. Further, these reactions reinforce the dominant ideology that views the young father's actions as laudable rather than expected. If these actions are expected, they are much more likely to be analyzed critically. A reaction free of the dominant ideology would deconstruct and interpret the value and the meaning of this event. When unexpected actions are not viewed critically, the illusion of change is easily created in the minds of people operating within the dominant ideology.

In the same vein, executives adopting participative management practices are often reinforced by consultants and employees for doing the unexpected—the laudable thing. The complete absence of democratic practices in manufacturing environments often prevents us from differentiating between the illusion of a transformed ideology and the authentic transformation of management philosophy and practice. An organization consultant must assist people in deconstructing the operating management philosophy so that the meanings of participative management practices can be critically assessed. This task, however, is not an easy one. When we are unreflective about the dominant ideology of our society, we have great difficulty analyzing and deconstructing our actions or the actions of others within the organization.

Consider, for example, the situation of the young husband and the dilemma it poses for his wife. If people are to know the truth—that her husband has only changed the child's diapers three times in ten months— the onus is on her to challenge the illusion of shared parenting. However, she may have difficulty doing so for several reasons. The dominant ideology reinforced in society is that men do not change babies—women do. The young wife, also submerged in this thinking, may feel that her husband is actually doing something for her that he does not have to do. This interpretation of the situation merely reflects her internalized acceptance of the dominant ideology that justifies men's natural sphere as public (work) and women's natural sphere as private (home and family). Even when women work, they have difficulty escaping this dominant ideology. Instead of challenging the equity of the situation, women who believe their primary responsibility is in the home strive to be superwomen. A complex intermingling of systems and values leads to this response. Cleo H. Cherryholmes (1988, p. 5) has noted that "ideology intertwines with power as individuals accept, believe, and internalize explanations and justifications for the asymmetries of their social world." Therefore, striving to be a superwoman is likely an internalized acceptance of a new ideology about the role of women in the world of work while simultaneously being trapped in the thinking of the dominant ideology which insists that a woman's place is in the home. Accepting one's lot does not remove the internalized anger and alienation, however.

In efforts to transform management philosophy, we encounter similar barriers. Many workers have learned "their place" in organizations. Consultants often find that workers believe management is making an effort to do something for them that it does not *have* to do. This thinking reflects their internalization of the dominant management ideology that assumes managers make decisions and workers carry them out. Any change from this ideology is unexpected and, therefore, often perceived as a gift. It is difficult for people to critically examine the value of a gift.

This situation is problematic for several reasons. Often organization consultants ask executives and workers to discuss the strengths and weaknesses of the participative management program or to delineate recommended changes. But if people are operating from within the dominant ideology of management, their expectations are constrained by the values of that ideology. Workers' expectations for inclusion in management decision making are so low that they are easily impressed with minimal participation in decisions and have limited expectations of true participation in an emergent participative management ideology.

Further, consultants who are asked to assess participative management practices encounter this same difficulty (albeit unknowingly). True participation in interpreting, assessing, and transforming the dominant management ideology requires emerged states of consciousness. Ann Schaef (1988) notes that "a raised consciousness . . . prevents us from overlooking what we might usually miss" (p. 212). People must engage in discussions that challenge their internalized beliefs about their rights and roles in organization decision making. When people are encouraged to analyze the values and beliefs operating in the dominant and emergent management ideologies, they become more sensitive to the disharmony between the organization's philosophy and actual practice.

Increased states of awareness, however, are not enough to escape the dominant ideology that often frames our thinking. If the mother of the young child in my previous example has sufficiently raised her consciousness to risk exposing her husband's shallow participation in parenting and challenge the illusion of equity, she may well be chastised by friends and relatives for being ungrateful for the "generous" (laudable rather than expected) help her husband does provide and may well be reminded of all the men who do nothing to help around the house. Experiences such as these tend to deny, suppress, and silence people's individual reality and create guilt in them for not being grateful for what little they do have. This reaction circumvents deeper investigation into the inequities of the existing ideology and leaves traditional beliefs and values safely intact. Catherine MacKinnon (1987) refers to this dominant ideology in our society as the most pervasive and tenacious system of power in history. Expressing discomfort with the dominant arrangement only to have one's reality dismissed creates internal confusion between what one is *told* is equitable and what one *feels* is equitable. It is this pernicious undermining of personal reality and the pressure to conform to the thinking of the dominant culture that keeps people from trusting, believing, and acting upon their own interpretations of life's experiences.

People caught in the confusion between personal reality and dominant ideology frequently suppress their own interpretations, concluding that their discomfort must lie in their own inadequacy. Marlene Packwood (1983, p. 11) has observed that "the basic structuring of the economic and political system is biased in favor of the dominant group and also because ideological hegemony is exercised by the dominant group, subordinate groups are often inhibited from being conscious of their oppression or from developing the confidence to fight that oppression." Recognizing that we function within a powerful dominant ideology that molds and constrains our thinking, we must ask: What do we truly assess when we assess submerged states of consciousness or, said differently, unconscious states of awareness? I contend that what is assessed is merely a reflected image of the dominant ideology of the organization.

Gareth Morgan (1986) believes that people live their lives as prisoners of their own past. Years of being reduced to machine parts on factory lines deskills people sufficiently to undermine confidence and deaden expectations. Morgan says that "Freud, Jung, and others see freedom as lying in an awareness of how the past influences the present through the unconscious" (p. 204). I believe that to free people of the "psychic prisons" that limit the authenticity of voices, thoughts, and aspirations, consultants must become skillful facilitators and educators for participative evaluation that deconstructs the management ideology undergirding participative management practices.

Claiming an Authentic Voice

When organization consultants are submerged in traditional management ideology, they tend to view critical assessment of participative practices as risky business. Cherryholmes (1988, p. 5) reminds us that people "seek to act in ways that are likely to be rewarded and avoid actions likely to be penalized." Organization consultants with a strong desire to please their clients (management) often function very conservatively within the confines of the organization's stated goals and objectives. This action is taken even when the social and political complexity of the environment mandates otherwise. Gareth Morgan (1986) argues: "Though managers and organization theorists often attempt to override this complexity by assuming that organizations are ultimately rational phenomena that must be understood with reference to their goals or objectives, this assumption often gets in the way of realistic analysis. If one truly wishes to understand an organization it is much wiser to start from the premise that organizations are complex, ambiguous, and paradoxical" (p. 322). The complexity of assessing efforts to transform management ideology must be brought to the forefront of evaluation methodology. Organization consultants must recognize that the forces of the dominant ideology, the interpretation of authentic participation, and the dilemmas of authentic voice in evaluation must become central to discussions with clients if management's philosophy is to be transformed and the intellectual, social, and psychological malaise of the organization's workers is to be addressed.

Most consultants to business and industry focus on establishing good relationships with their clients and are very careful to posture themselves appropriately. Consultants, as well as internal evaluators, fear raising unpopular questions because they fear the personal and professional rejection that might follow. Therefore, consultants typically remain silent on issues of authentic participation, authentic voice, and equity for all stakeholders unless these issues are raised by the client. Most consultants opt to function conservatively within scripted roles and a "don't make waves" mentality. Anne Schaef (1988, p. 113) notes that people in decision-making positions are not willing to "risk the ire of powerful elements of the organization in order to make the organization congruent with its own mission and purpose." Maxine Greene (1990, p. 2) observes that "there is a general withdrawal from what ought to be public concerns. Messages and announcements fill the air; but there is, because of the withdrawal, a widespread speechlessness—a silence where there might be, where there ought to be, an impassioned and significant dialogue." Organization consultants are often participants in that silence.

What is needed is greater moral courage on the part of organization consultants who design and assess participative management initiatives. This "widespread speechlessness" must be given a voice in evaluation methodology. We need consultants who view their primary responsibility as raising unpopular questions that others fear to raise, making uncomfortable observations that may challenge the illusion on management transformation, and leading people through passionate and significant dialogues about the assumptions and interests that undergird the roles, rights, and responsibilities of people in organizations.

Through critical, open dialogue, people can achieve greater clarity about the realities and myths of the management ideology they are collectively creating and reinforcing. Introspection and personal reflection allow us to emerge from the dominant ideology that imprisons our thinking. This statement is as true for CEOs as it is for line workers. Business executives benefit greatly from this kind of personal and public reflection.

The research of Leonard Silk, an economist and journalist, and David Vogel, a business school professor, offers considerable insight into the concerns of business leaders. Silk and Vogel were invited to attend the National Industrial Conference Board, a prestigious representative association for large businesses that typically greets 360 executives from more than 260 organizations. Following this conference, Silk and Vogel (1977, p. 32) wrote about those proceedings and conversations. In their book *Ethics and Profits: The Crisis of Confidence in American Business,* they noted that "American business leaders are very concerned about understanding their role in society. Like all individuals, they want to have a clear sense of what their particular function is and how it fits into the overall goals and needs of the social system of which they are a part. They want to believe that what they are doing with their lives is appropriate and useful." Business leaders, like most people, do not reflect upon the role they play in reinforcing the dominant ideology of organizations—or upon the impact this ideology has on the lives of the people with whom they work. The opportunity to bring the actions of the organization in line with its espoused philosophy will appeal greatly to many progressive, sincere leaders in business and industry.

Clearly, it is easier to conduct a surface-level evaluation of participative management initiatives because it is less threatening (and more traditional) to focus on issues of efficiency and effectiveness than issues of philosophy and ideology. The latter can be quite discomforting. However, failure to assess and deconstruct participative initiatives within the context of the dominant ideology fails to obtain the depth of inquiry necessary for making a major shift in the philosophy and practices of people within the organization. A shift in management philosophy and practice requires that both evaluators and participants move to a deeper level of involvement in participative evaluation by engaging in a personal inquiry into the organization, the roles and rights of its people, and the meaning of authentic participation. This focus enables each participant to deconstruct the operating system of thought in the organization through her or his own interpretations, as well as from the reflections of others. This exploration calls for a much deeper and broader interpretation of what it means to evaluate a phenomenon as complex as the transformation of management philosophy and practice. Delahanty and Gemill (1982) call for an exploration of the "black hole" of organization life that swallows and traps the rich energies of people. Similarly, Dewey (1934) expresses concern about people's attentiveness to the realities of their own lived lives. These efforts require liberating education, mediation, and facilitation.

I propose that viewing participative management initiatives as a transformation in ideology rather than a change in technique takes participative evaluation one crucial step further. This focus lifts the fog of the dominant ideology that clouds our ability to think clearly about the world of work we have created. This process must make people genuine participants with an authentic voice in identifying, interpreting, and analyzing the barriers that impede authentic participation in organizations. To do that, we must critically examine the dominant management ideology of the organization so that we may finally put an end to praising and reinforcing the *illusion* of change in management philosophy and practice.

References

Baloff, N., and Doherty, M. "Potential Pitfalls in Employee Participation." *Organizational Dynamics*, 1989, *17*, (3), 51–62.

Barra, R. *Putting Quality Circles to Work.* New York: McGraw-Hill, 1983.

Belenky, M. F., and others. *Women's Ways of Knowing.* New York: Basic Books, 1986.

Boudon, R. *The Analysis of Ideology.* Chicago: University of Chicago Press, 1990.

Chandler, A. D. *Strategy and Structure.* Cambridge, Mass.: MIT Press, 1962.

Cherryholmes, C. *Power and Criticism.* New York: Teachers College Press, 1988.

Delahanty, F., and Gemill, G. "The Black Hole in Group Development." Paper presented at the Academy of Management Meetings, New York, 1982.

Dewey, J. *Art as Experience.* New York: Capricorn, 1934.

Follett, M. P. *Dynamic Administration.* London: Pitman, 1941.

Greene, M. *The Dialectic of Freedom.* New York: Teachers College Press, 1990.

Howard, R. *Brave New Workplace.* New York: Penguin Books, 1985.

Jacques, E. "In Praise of Hierarchy." *Harvard Business Review*, 1990, *1*, 127–133.

Kanter, R. M. *Changemasters.* New York: Simon & Schuster, 1983.

Lawler, E., and Mohrman, S. "Quality Circles: After the Honeymoon." *Organizational Dynamics*, Spring 1987, pp. 42–54.

McCarthy, T. *The Critical Theory of Jürgen Habermas.* Cambridge, Mass.: Harvard University Press, 1978.

McGregor, D. *The Human Side of the Enterprise.* New York: McGraw-Hill, 1960.

MacKinnon, C. *Feminism Unmodified.* Cambridge, Mass.: Harvard University Press, 1987.

Mayo, E. *The Human Problems of the Industrial Civilization.* New York: Macmillan, 1933.

Morgan, G. *Images of Organizations.* Newbury Park, Calif.: Sage, 1986.

Packwood, M. "The Colonel's Lady and Judy O'Grady—Sisters Under the Skin?" *Trouble and Strife*, 1983, *1*, 7–12.

Peters, T. *Thriving on Chaos.* New York: Knopf, 1987.

Peters, T., and Waterman, R. *In Search of Excellence.* New York: Harper & Row, 1982.

Pugh, D. S. *Writers on Organizations.* Newbury Park, Calif.: Sage, 1965.

Schaef, A. *The Addictive Organization.* San Francisco: Harper & Row, 1988.

Schoenberger, R. J. *Japanese Manufacturing Techniques.* New York: Free Press, 1982.

Silk, L., and Vogel, D. *Ethics and Profits: The Crisis of Confidence in American Business.* New York: Simon & Schuster, 1977.

Sirotnik, K., and Oakes, J. "Evaluation as Critical Inquiry: School Improvement as a Case in Point." In K. Sirotnik (ed.), *Evaluation and Social Justice: Issues in Public Education.* New Directions for Program Evaluation, no. 45. San Francisco: Jossey-Bass, 1990.

Thompson, M. S. *Benefit-Cost Analysis for Program Evaluation.* Newbury Park, Calif.: Sage, 1980.

Zand, D. E. "Collateral Organization: A New Strategy." In W. French and C. Bell (eds.), *Organization Development.* Homewood, Ill.: BPI/Irwin, 1989.

Colleen L. Larson joined the faculty in School Administration at Indiana University after having spent six years as an organization consultant to Fortune 500 companies. Her research interests include evaluation theory, organizational culture, and the use of photography and metaphors in interpreting evaluation information.

INDEX

Academic sector, qualitative research methods in the, 42, 44–45
Acquisitions, business. *See* Mergers, acquisitions, and takeovers
Advertising and market research, 42–43
Alice in Wonderland environment, the, 7–8
Alienation of individuals, 57, 67
Alkin, M. C., 5, 6, 11, 12, 13
Amado, G., 58, 62
Amy, D. J., 64–65, 70
Andrews, K. R., 68, 71
Antilla, S., 43, 48
Argyris, C., 9, 13, 55, 61
Arthur Andersen & Co., 22–24
Artifacts, cultural, 9, 10
Assumptions of an organization. *See* Culture, organizational
Asymmetries, social world, 80–81
AT&T Quality Steering Committee, 31, 39

Background information, knowing client, 18, 20–21
Bailey, R. W., 29, 30, 39
Behavior, human. *See* Human nature; User-oriented product evaluation
Bellenger, D. N., 43, 48
Benefit plans, employee, 46
Benefits of evaluation: features *vs.*, 18, 19–20; presenting the, 21–22
Benimoff, N. I., 36, 39
Berger, M. A., 10, 13
Bergsrud, F., 46, 48
Bernhardt, K. L., 43, 48
Bernstein, L., 47, 48
Bischoff, R. N., 46, 48
Boudon, R., 76, 85
Boundaries, permeability of, 52, 54, 59
Brandenburg, D. C., 65, 71
Braskamp, L. A., 5, 13
Brethower, D. M., 66, 71
Brinkerhoff, R. O., 19, 25, 65–66, 71
Bryant, F. B., 53–54, 55, 61
Burton, J., 43–44, 48
Business strategy: aligning evaluation proposals with, 20–22, 65–66; as

amoral, 66–67; the rational framework of, 52–54; through structure, 75–79

Calingo, L.M.R., 53–54, 55, 61
Caplan, N., 5, 13
Casey, M. A., 46, 47, 48
Catalyst's Corporate Child Care Resource, 46
Chandler, A. D., 75, 85
Change, organizational: cracking the illusion of, 79–82; cultural, 11–12; magnitude of American, 1, 7–8; nature of inquiry into, 2; parallel structures and, 75–79
Cherryholmes, C. H., 80–81, 82, 85
Child-care services, 46
Clark, D. L., 53, 54, 62
Client organizations: benefits of evaluation for, 18, 19–20; evaluation and the reputation of, 19–20; identifying major issues affecting, 22–23, 79–82; life cycle of, 23–24; motivating action by, 21–22; presentations to, 21–22; understanding the, 18, 20–21, 82–84
Collateral organization structures, 76–79
Comparison of organizations, cultural, 10
Computer technology: development phases, 34–37; issues of quality in, 29–30, 32–34; measuring the quality of, 30–31; methodologies for evaluation of, 31–32, 37
Concept definition and testing, high-tech product, 34–37
Conformance testing, product, 34–35
Consumer perceptions and market research, 42–43
Contexts, cultural. *See* Culture, organizational; Environments of organizations
Coordinative evaluation, 54
Cost reduction, evaluation features and, 19
County agents (USDA), 46
Cousins, 6, 14
Cox, K. C., 43–44, 48
Croquet game analogy, 7–8
Crosby, P. B., 28, 39

Ordering Information

NEW DIRECTIONS FOR PROGRAM EVALUATION is a series of paperback books that presents the latest techniques and procedures for conducting useful evaluation studies of all types of programs. Books in the series are published quarterly in Fall, Winter, Spring, and Summer and are available for purchase by subscription as well as by single copy.

SUBSCRIPTIONS for 1991 cost $48.00 for individuals (a savings of 20 percent over single-copy prices) and $70.00 for institutions, agencies, and libraries. Please do not send institutional checks for personal subscriptions. Standing orders are accepted.

SINGLE COPIES cost $15.95 when payment accompanies order. (California, New Jersey, New York, and Washington, D.C., residents please include appropriate sales tax.) Billed orders will be charged postage and handling.

DISCOUNTS FOR QUANTITY ORDERS are available. Please write to the address below for information.

ALL ORDERS must include either the name of an individual or an official purchase order number. Please submit your order as follows:
   Subscriptions: specify series and year subscription is to begin
   Single copies: include individual title code (such as PE1)

MAIL ALL ORDERS TO:
   Jossey-Bass Inc., Publishers
   350 Sansome Street
   San Francisco, California 94104

FOR SALES OUTSIDE OF THE UNITED STATES CONTACT:
   Maxwell Macmillan International Publishing Group
   866 Third Avenue
   New York, New York 10022

OTHER TITLES AVAILABLE IN THE
NEW DIRECTIONS FOR PROGRAM EVALUATION SERIES
Nick L. Smith, *Editor-in-Chief*